American Community Colleges: The International Student's Guide

C.J. Shane

Rope's End Publishing
P.O. Box 13689
Tucson, AZ 85732

© copyright 2017 Rope's End Publishing
All Rights Reserved
ISBN: 978-0-9892216-2-7

Live as if you were to die tomorrow. Learn as if you were to live forever. ~~ Mahatma Gandhi

NOTES about Footnotes at the end of chapters.

---A WINWOOD security box appears when you click on some Footnote links. You are asked for your name and password. This is for currently-enrolled students. If you see this WINWOOD box, just click on "Cancel" to access the website directly.

---Links ending with "PDF" often come with an automatic warning about viruses.

CONTENTS

Introduction 7

1 American Education and the Community College 12

2 Choosing a Community College 26

3 Applying to a Community College 45

4 Visas and Additional Forms 58

5 Welcome to the U.S.A. 68

6 Academics and Student Life 76

7 Living in the U.S.A. 89

8 American People and Culture 108

9 Profiles of Community Colleges 121

10 International Students Speak 155

11 Glossary of Terms 176

Index 187

Photo Credits 195

Acknowledgements/About the Author 196

INTRODUCTION

A degree from an American university is highly prized in countries around the world. An American university degree is considered to be a ticket to a better job, higher wages, and a brighter future. Earning a degree is an important step along the path to creating a better life for yourself and for your family as well.

International students typically choose an American university for its academic reputation in the field that the student wants to study. International students often make important professional connections at their universities that later will serve them well in their careers. The most popular fields of study for international students are: 1) business, finance, and management; 2) engineering; 3) math and computer science; and 4) social sciences.

We find proof in the numbers. According to *U.S. News and World Report*, a record number of 886,052 undergraduate and graduate international students came to the U.S. to study in the 2013-2014 school year, a growth of 72% since 2000. Of these, almost one-third (31%) came from one country, the People's Republic of China. There are currently growth surges in the number of students from Kuwait, Brazil, and Saudi Arabia. India and South Korea also send significant numbers to the U.S. to study. California, New York and Texas are the states that host the greatest number of international students. The four universities that now have the greatest number of international students are New York University, the University of Southern California, the University of Illinois Urbana-Champaign, and Columbia University. (1)

Two-thirds of these international students will seek a degree in a **STEM field** (science, technology, engineering, mathematics) or in a business-related field such as management or marketing.

Nearly half (45%) will extend their visas to work in the same location as their college or university under the **Optional Practical Training (OPT)** program. (2)

And yet, the rewards of earning a degree from an American institution of higher learning are offset by the challenges involved. A university education is expensive, and students must find funds to pay for tuition and living expenses for at least four years of study. Students must go through a detailed application process to gain entry to their university of choice. Before even arriving on campus, students are required to go through a rigorous visa application to gain entry into the U.S. There are many forms to fill out and interviews to pass, and great attention to detail is required at every step of the visa process.

For many years, most international students seeking a bachelor's degree went directly into a four-year college or university in the United States. However, it has become apparent that this path has some disadvantages.

In recent years tuition has become more and more expensive at four-year universities. American students often leave school with a huge debt despite access to financial aid and scholarships. This access to financial aid is not easily available to international students, and scholarships at the undergraduate level are very difficult to obtain. Many four-year campuses are large and flooded with thousands of students. Classes can be very large, sometimes with as many as 500 students.

Getting help with enhancing English language skills is a challenge, too. International students often feel lost in the crowd, not always knowing how to proceed or where to get help. They often find themselves in a very unfamiliar situation just after arriving from their home countries. Culture shock can be dramatic and difficult. Loneliness and homesickness are common, and understanding the nuances of American college can seem impossible. Not all students can overcome these challenges. They become very discouraged, and withdraw from the university.

Ready for my class!

Because of the many challenges of starting at a four-year American university, more and more international students have chosen in recent years to attend a community college for their first two years of American education. Then after graduating from community college, they transfer to a four-year institution to finish their bachelor's degree. Many of the problems encountered by international students on large university campuses don't exist or are fewer when studying at a two-year community college. Because of this, more and more international students are choosing this higher education alternative.

A two-year associate degree from a community college is the first step toward academic success and a pathway to a bachelor's degree. These days this is often referred to as a **2+2 degree**

program. Students who graduate from a community college are less likely to drop out of a four-year university and are more likely to finish their bachelor's degree. Community college students demonstrate to potential employers that they are determined, committed, and responsible learners with better-than-average skills.

The degree earned at a community college frequently leads to a desirable job at graduation, or a better job while studying for a four-year degree. In recent years as many as one in five community college students already have bachelor's degrees. Either they couldn't find a job in their chosen field or they wanted a better job than the one they had. So they returned to community college to get the specific skills needed for better employment in a new field. Nursing and computer science are especially attractive fields for these students.

For all these reasons, more and more international students are seriously considering spending two years in a community college as their first American educational experience.

This book is a guide to the American community college system for international students. We will cover the following topics:

- how community colleges fit into the U.S. system of higher education
- the advantages for you as an international student to start your American education in a community college
- the steps you must go through to study at a U.S. community college
- key factors that you must consider when choosing an American community college
- the process of applying to and gaining entrance into a community college
- the process of applying for a U.S. visa
- the forms needed when arriving in the U.S. and passing through U.S. customs

- choosing classes at your new college and how to register for those classes
- how to get help improving your English-language skills
- basics about living in America, including housing, transportation, and medical care
- American culture and how to deal with culture shock

As we go through this guide, we'll be referring to programs and policies at specific colleges. This will give us examples to make it easier to understand how these programs work and what the results will be for studying in a specific program.

Finally, in a series of profiles, we'll take a closer look at several American community colleges, and we'll review what these colleges have to offer you. We'll learn about support for students in areas such as tutoring, including English language learning; support for daily life issues such as housing, transportation, and health care; and activities that enhance quality of life for the college students. We'll look at how each college manages its students' transfer to four year colleges and what kinds of transfer programs and partnerships the community college has established.

Let's get started!

Footnotes and Links: Introduction

(1) *US News.* "Number of International College Students Continues to Climb, http://www.usnews.com/education/best-colleges/articles/2014/11/17/number-of-international-college-students-continues-to-climb?int=981408
(2) Brookings.edu. *The Geography of Foreign Students in U.S. Higher Education: Origins and Destinations.* http://www.brookings.edu/research/interactives/2014/geography-of-foreign-students#/M10420

Chapter 1. American Education and the Community College

Let's start first with an overview of the American system of education and see where community colleges fit into this system. You might think that the U.S. federal (national) government controls and administers public education in the U.S. Not so. Actually the individual states and local communities have much more control over public education than does the federal government. Each state's education department and the town or county's local school districts are responsible for administering and regulating public education. As a result, requirements vary somewhat from district to district and from state to state. There are approximately 15,000 school districts in the U.S.

K-12 Education

The U.S. public education system is often referred to as K-12 education. Kindergarten is the first step in the K-12 system. Kindergarten starts for children at age five. Students attend kindergarten classes to learn skills they will need when they start elementary school at age six. The K-12 system ends with the final year of high school, grade 12. Students are typically 17 or 18 when they graduate from high school.

Public education for children from elementary through high school is funded by citizens living in the same district as the school is located. In most cases, local citizens pay a tax on the property that they own. The property is usually a house or some land. That's why it is called "public education" – because the public pays for it.

There are also privately-owned and privately-funded schools. Many private schools are owned by religious organizations that may provide financial support. Other secular private schools charge each student a tuition fee which the parents pay. Examples of privately-owned schools are Montessori schools and Waldorf schools.

Note that there are educational opportunities for children even before kindergarten although these are not part of the public education system. Pre-school is a nursery school for children who are too young to go to public elementary school. Children are not required by the state or local district to attend a pre-school. Today many parents work during the day. Consequently, many children are placed in a pre-school or nursery school where they both play and learn while their parents are at work. Children that need care while parents are working can also go to "day care" where they receive care, but little instruction.

Elementary school may begin with kindergarten at age five and continue with grades one through six (ages six through 12 years). Depending on the school district, children go on to "middle school" for grades seven and eight, or "junior high," with grades seven, eight and nine. This is followed by high school grades nine or ten through 12 (ages 15-18).

Learning is fun!

Attendance for all students in public schools is compulsory starting at age six when students enter the first grade. Kindergarten is compulsory in some states but not in others. Public school is compulsory until the age of 16 or 17 depending on each state's requirement. Students are not legally required to graduate from high school. Many students drop out of school without finishing. Later they have the option of attending special classes and passing tests in order to earn a GED. **GED** refers to either General Education Development or General Education Diploma, and it is equivalent to a high school diploma. Some community colleges offer GED classes.

Upon graduation from high school, students have the choice of a) seeking employment immediately; b) attending a technical school for specialized training; or c) continuing in the public/private education system to seek higher degrees at a two-year community college or a four-year university. After receiving a bachelor's degree, students may continue to study for a master's and a doctoral degree. They may also enter law, medical, dental, or veterinary school.

This gives you an overview of the educational system in the U.S. starting with pre-school and kindergarten and going all the way through graduate and professional degree programs. You will be attending classes with American students, most of whom went through the public education system described here.

Now let's take a closer look at community colleges.

Community Colleges and Technical Schools

There are more than 4,000 accredited post-secondary institutions of learning in the United States. Of this total, nearly 1,200 are known as community colleges. Approximately 12.4 million students study at community colleges in the United States.

The term "**community college**" has different meanings in different countries. In the United States, a community college is a two-year institution of higher learning. In the past, American community colleges were called "junior colleges," and you will still see that term used. Community colleges offer fundamental academic courses that prepare a student for transfer to a college or university where students study for a four-year bachelor's degree. Students on the associate degree path are required to take introductory courses such as English composition, math, science, and social sciences. They also take courses in their area of interest such as business administration, computer-information technology, history or psychology. These classes prepare students for more advanced classes at a four-year college or university.

The academic degrees earned at a community college are called **associate degrees**. The degree may be an Associate of Arts (AA), Associate of Science (AS), or Associate of Applied Science (AAS). After earning the associate degree, students have the option of transferring to a college or university that offers bachelor's degree programs.

The term "**technical college**" is another term that applies to two-year colleges. Technical colleges are oriented toward preparing students for employment immediately upon graduation. Another term you will encounter for this type of education is "vocational." Technical and vocational training study courses are found in all the major fields, including medicine, computer technology, business, and trades.

Examples of technical training include the following jobs: accounting assistant or bookkeeper, nursing assistant, dental hygienist, para-legal assistant, veterinary assistant, hotel manager, emergency medical technician, retail-store manager, electrician, plumber, computer-aided drafting technician, website designer, and solar panel installation technician. When a student graduates from this technical/vocational program, he/she will earn a **certificate** and then begin looking for a job in his/her chosen field. Individuals who already have earned a bachelor's degree can study for a certificate in education to become employed as a certified teacher.

Training to be veterinary assistants at Austin Community College

Earning a certificate often takes less time than earning an associate degree which usually requires two years of study. Students may seek only a certificate or they can seek a certificate and at the same time, they can also study for an associate degree. For example, Cabrillo College in California offers an associate degree in Computer Networking and System Administration (CNSA). At the same time, students can earn a certificate in Cybersecurity Fundamentals. (1)

Community colleges and technical colleges are often combined together at the same college. Many students take the associate degree path while others study for a technical certificate. Some students take both academic and technical classes. They can seek employment upon graduating with their technical certificate. Later, they may decide to transfer to a university with the intention of earning a bachelor's degree. They can do this if they also earned an associate degree at the community college.

Community colleges often offer classes to earn a GED (general education diploma), mentioned earlier as an alternative to a high school degree. Also offered at many community colleges are classes for professionals who have already earned a bachelor's degree. In these classes, professionals earn **continuing education units (CEU)** to help them stay current in their professions. Many community colleges also offer advanced certificate programs for professionals who are interested in advancing their skills.

Let's look at some additional examples.

Austin Community College (Austin, Texas) has several degree and certificate options, too. If you are interested in accounting, you can earn an associate degree, and then continue at a four-year university to earn a bachelor's degree in accounting. Or you can earn a certificate as an accounting clerk qualified to begin working after earning the certificate. Or you may be interested in an advanced professional certificate which requires that you already have a bachelor's degree. (2)

Bunker Hill Community College in Boston, Massachusetts also offers both associate degree and certificate programs. Are you interested in becoming a music teacher? You can earn an associate degree at Bunker Hill, then transfer to finish your bachelor's degree in music at a four-year college or university. (3) Or perhaps you plan to earn an associate degree in computer science, then transfer to a four-year university and earn a bachelor's degree in computer science. While you are at Bunker Hill CC, you discover a special certification program available in Microsoft applications. Becoming a Microsoft Applications Support Specialist at Bunker Hill means you'll get practical training in this certificate program as well as theoretical education in your academic classes. (4)

Or perhaps your home country has a rapidly-developing solar industry. Your ultimate goal is to earn a bachelor's degree in engineering. However, you want some hands-on experience. Colorado Mountain College has a certificate program in Basic Solar Photovoltaic Installation that will give you that hands-on experience. (5)

After earning the associate degree, community-college students transfer to a four-year university or college to seek a bachelor's degree. This is one path to a university bachelor's degree. The other path is for students to go directly from high school to a four-year university and begin their first year, called the **freshman year**, at the university. Students who transfer from a community college with an associate degree start at a four-year college or university in the third year which is called the **junior year**. The four years of university education are freshman, sophomore, junior, and senior years.

Upon earning a bachelor's degree, many graduates seek employment. Or they may decide to continue their education by going on for a higher graduate degree such as a master's degree (two years) and then a doctoral/PhD degree (at least three years). Or they can seek a professional degree such as a law degree or a medical degree.

Typically community colleges provide education primarily for students from the nearby community. However many community colleges are very welcoming to international students and have active recruitment programs targeting students from around the world.

Why Choose to Study at a Community College?

Lower Costs

Probably the most cited reason for choosing an American community college is that tuition and fees are almost always much lower than at a four-year university. Saving money at the undergraduate level means that students will have more funds available for higher education. That is, those students who intend to continue on for a bachelor's degree or graduate degrees (master's, PhD) will have the advantage of having spent less on their first two years of American education at a community college.

Also, the lower fees and tuition means that higher education in the U.S. is possible for the first time for many students who come from middle-class families in the developing countries. The *Los Angeles Times* reported in late 2015 that lower middle-class families in China can seriously consider an American education for their sons and daughters if they attend a community college. (6).

Let's look at some cost comparisons. Keep in mind that public colleges and universities typically charge **in-state tuition** for students who are legal residents of the state where the college is located. If a student comes from another state or from another country, the student must pay **out-of-state tuition**.

Austin Community College in Austin, Texas, charges out-of-state and international students $ 1,080 (2016) for a three-credit hour course. (7) In the same city, Austin, Texas, the University of Texas charges students different fees depending upon the course of study. For a three-credit hour undergraduate course, out-of-state students pay $ 8,392 for business courses; $7,927 for engineering courses; and $7,323 for **liberal arts** course. (figures from 2016) (8)

Another financial factor to consider is the **cost of living**. The cost of living includes apartment rent, **utilities** (gas, electricity, water), food costs, transportation costs and more. These costs are linked more to the physical location of the college than to college financial policies. Some cities in the U.S. are far more expensive to live in than others. New York City, for example, is the most expensive city in the U.S. with Honolulu and San Francisco close behind. Keep the cost-of-living in mind when choosing a college. We'll discuss cost-of-living in depth in Chapter 2.

Expanded Academic Options and Support

Smaller class sizes are typical in community colleges. If you are in a class of only 25 students, you'll have more opportunities to get to know and talk with your professor. You'll have a chance to ask questions directly of the professor, and get help when you need it. Also you'll have more opportunities to interact with your fellow classmates in smaller classes. You'll have a greater chance of forming friendships. In a large university with classes that can have up to 500 students, interaction with professors and fellow students is much more difficult.

Professors in four-year and graduate-school universities are obligated to do research and publish academic papers. This focus on research and publishing often takes the professors away from their teaching. Community colleges, on the other hand, put the focus on good teaching. Research and publishing are secondary considerations. You, the student, will benefit from the focus on teaching.

Community colleges often have the latest technology to enhance learning in technical areas. After all, many students are there to become certified in a specific technical area. The college is responsible for training these students in the most up-to-date technology.

Even a quick look at many community college course catalogs reveals a large number of courses available to students in a wide range of fields. There are often hundreds of programs to choose from, both for associate degree programs and for certification programs. Because of the wide choice of programs, and the options for skills-based education, community colleges have become attractive to individuals who want to become more employable, or to change careers entirely. *U.S. News and World Report* found in October, 2015, that one in every 14 students at a community college had a bachelor's degree.

Community colleges very frequently provide academic support for your classes, especially for English-language learning. Some community colleges also have more flexible English-language requirements. This means that when you enter the community college, you may not speak English at the level needed for four-year university. With the flexible requirements at a community college, English language tutoring support, and informal opportunities to converse with American classmates, you'll be able to increase your English-language skills before transferring to a large university.

Disabled students may qualify for extra support in the form of special software or equipment to help them. Tutors are often available to help learning-disabled students, as are sign-language interpreters for deaf students, and computers with speech synthesis capability for blind students.

Transfer Partnerships

Community colleges have developed strong **transfer partnerships** with four-year universities. These are sometimes called **articulation agreements**. A transfer partnership indicates that your acceptance into a partner university is guaranteed, provided that you have met all the academic qualifications. If your scores and final grades in your community college classes are sufficient, transferring credits for those courses to a partner institution is guaranteed. This transfer will be easier than attempting to move to a non-partner university. Most community college websites give a list of transfer partnerships.

Keep in mind, too, that top-level universities are more likely to accept you if you've already proven yourself at a local community college.

Community colleges generally provide a better learning and living environment for students. You are much more likely to get help with personal issues such as finding a job at a community college than at a large university.

Employment Opportunities

Many community colleges have a program called **Optional Practical Training (OPT)**. Provided you have maintained your status at the college, you may be eligible for a temporary job in a field related to your **major** area of study. This option is available only to F-1 visa students, and only after completing one year of academic study. For example, Pima Community College in Tucson, Arizona, has facilitated OPT placement in Tucson high-tech firms for students in business and graphics fields.

21

A Chance to Experience American Life and American Culture

Life is about more than just earning a degree. Yes, you are planning on studying in America to earn a degree. However, you are also a student in the United States so you can learn about American life and American culture. This is part of becoming a complete and developed person – to learn as much as you can about many things.

Americans love sports, so if you also love sports, you'll have opportunities to play on a team or to attend big games with your fellow students. If you love outdoor activities such as bicycling, hiking, or snow skiing, you'll find opportunities for these activities as well. Do you like film, or poetry, or art? Or maybe you are interested in computers? Student groups exist for these activities, too.

Learning about American culture and life can be very professionally rewarding and lucrative as well. Imagine that you want to study international business. Your goal is to return to your home country and help local businesses to create business partnerships with firms in the U.S. A working knowledge of American culture and life will be invaluable in this endeavor.

Steps to Studying at an American Community College

What follows is a summary of the steps you take to study at an American community college. We'll go into more detail in later chapters. The first step – research, plan, learn as much as you can – is the most important because it is the foundation for everything that follows.

Research, Plan, Learn as Much as You Can

The first step – research, plan, learn as much as you can – is the most important because it is the foundation for everything that follows. Many international students make a big mistake by not being prepared. They fail to do the research needed to determine which college is right for them, which course of study to follow, how to apply and gain admission to a college, and to take care of all the bureaucratic details required to gain entry into the U.S., into your college, and into a successful educational experience.

Currently, we have access to a huge amount of information on the internet. You can look closely at the websites of thousands of colleges in the U.S. and learn very specific details about what each college offers. You also have the option of emailing the college contact staff person, and asking questions of that person.

In the following chapters, we'll look at all these topics. You'll begin to understand what you need to look for on a college website. You'll learn what questions you need to ask and what details to focus on.

Don't forget! Research is fundamental to planning. Learn as much as you can before you ever leave home.

Select Your College

Again, this is where doing your research comes in. You should consider several factors when choosing a college. First, you want to make sure that your college is both accredited by regional educational agencies responsible for evaluating academic standards, and also certified by the Student and Exchange Visitor Program (SEVP). You want your college to be strong academically in your field of study, and you want your course credits to transfer to the four-year college or university where you will earn your bachelor's degree.

There are other factors, too. Do you already have a four-year university selected where you want to study for a bachelor's degree? You'll need to know the transfer options at your community college.

There are other considerations such as choosing where in the U.S. you want to live. Cost of living is an important factor. Some cities are much more expensive to live in than others. Weather is a factor. Cultural and sporting opportunities are things to think about, too. You'll spend several years living in the United States. What kind of experience do you want to have?

See Chapter 2 for more about selecting a community college.

Get Your Passport
Passports are issued by your home national government. Each nation has different procedures for acquiring a passport.

Apply for Admission to Your College
Each community college website has detailed information about its own application process. See Chapter 3 for more information about the application process.

Apply for a Visa
Applying for a visa is a big job! It usually means filling out a lot of paperwork, getting transcripts, proving you have enough financial resources to live and study in the U.S. There may be additional forms you have to provide, and you'll likely be required to go for an interview at a U.S. Embassy in your home country. See Chapters 4 and 5 for information about visas, additional forms, and easy passage through customs at U.S. ports of entry.

~~~

These are the beginning steps. After you've arrived in the United States, you'll have other things to think about such as registering for classes, living in the U.S., cultural topics, and more. We'll also take a look at transferring to a four-year university after your graduation from a community college. We'll cover all those things in later chapters. Then we'll look at profiles of some community colleges around the U.S. so you can see how it all works.

Footnotes and Links: Chapter 1

(1). Cabrillo College. Computer and Information Systems. https://www.cabrillo.edu/academics/cis/

(2) Austin Community College. All Credit Degrees and Certificates. http://www.austincc.edu/degrees-and-certificates/explore-educational-choices/all-credit-degrees-and-certificates

(3) Bunker Hill Community College. Programs of Study, 2015-2017. http://www.bhcc.mass.edu/programsofstudy/index.php

(4) Bunker Hill Community College. Microsoft Applications Support Specialist Certificate Program. http://bhcc.mass.edu/programsofstudy/programs/microsoftapplicationssupportspecialist/

(5) Colorado Mountain College. Solar Energy. http://coloradomtn.edu/programs/solar_energy/

(6) Los Angeles Times. *Not Only China's Wealthy Want to Study in America.* December 28, 2015. http://www.latimes.com/local/california/la-me-chinese-students-20151228-story.html

(7) Austin Community College. Tuition and Fees Chart. http://www.austincc.edu/tuition-and-financial-aid/tuition-and-fees-chart

(8) University of Texas at Austin. Traditional Tuition. http://www.utexas.edu/tuition/costs.html

Chapter 2. Choosing a Community College

There are over 1,100 community colleges in the United States. With so many to choose from, finding the right college for you is important. Selecting a community college requires defining your goals in advance, then doing quality research to find which college is best for achieving those goals. Make a list of your five or even ten top community colleges that appear to help you to achieve your goals. Learn everything you can about each college on your list. American community colleges typically have extensive websites with a huge amount of information. So go to the web first, search in the English language, and find those colleges that look best for your personal situation. Then narrow your choice down to two or three colleges.

A summary of factors you will consider when choosing a community college:

- knowing your academic and career goals;
- determining the certification and accreditation of your chosen community college;
- learning about transfer partnerships between your community college and your chosen four-year college or university;
- learning the costs of college tuition and fees;
- learning what college support is available for international students, including English-language training or tutoring;
- learning about the location of the college within the United States, including considerations of weather, cost-of-living (costs of rent, transportation and food costs), and cultural opportunities.

- learning if the community college is friendly toward international students and actively recruiting international students. Such a college will be more desirable than one that shows little interest in international students. The friendliness factor is usually very apparent on the college's website.

Your Academic and Career Goals

Start your search for the best community college by considering your professional goals. What kind of employment do you want after graduation? Do you want to complete your education ready to enter a field related to computer technology? Or international business? Or a medical field? The fashion industry? The film industry? Before you apply to a community college, you will want to have a good idea of what your final goal will be.

When you have answered that question, the next step is to look for a four-year college or university. Look for a university with a bachelor's degree program that will help you achieve your career goal. Then find a community college that will lead you to the four-year university that supports your career and academic goals.

A good resource for rankings of four-year American colleges is the *Best Colleges and Rankings List* from *U.S. News* (1) Note that in addition to overall academic ranking of colleges and universities, there are also specialized rankings such *as Best Undergraduate Business Programs* and *Best Undergraduate Engineering Programs*. ("**Undergraduate**" refers to a four-year program leading to a bachelor's degree). There's even a list of colleges with the most international students. These rankings are very helpful when choosing a four-year college to complete your bachelor's degree.

Community colleges offer classes in standard academic fields such as basic biology and chemistry, English composition, and world history or U.S. history. Often these academic courses will be required for a four-year bachelor's degree. You will transfer these credits to your university when you are ready to go on for your bachelor's degree.

In addition to standard academic courses, community colleges often specialize in a specific field, and will offer courses in that field. For example, Valencia College in Orlando, Florida has both an associate degree program and a certificate program in Film Production Technology. World-famous film director Steven Spielberg has said that Valencia's film program is one of the best anywhere. (2)

U.S. News and World Report is well-known for its extensive publications on American education. On the *U.S. News* website devoted to community colleges, you can search by state, and then by the name of the college. The next step is to go to the community college's website and start your research about that college. (3)

Accreditation and SEVP Certification

Accreditation

You want to be certain that your community college is both accredited and **SEVP certified**. Let's look at **accreditation** first. According to the U.S. Department of Education, "Accreditation is the recognition that an institution maintains standards requisite for its graduates to gain admission to other reputable institutions of higher learning or to achieve credentials for professional practice. The goal of accreditation is to ensure that education provided by institutions of higher education meets acceptable levels of quality." (4) There are several accrediting agencies in different regions of the U.S.

Accreditation is crucial because your earned course credits may not transfer to a four-year institution if those credits were earned at a non-accredited community college. Keep in mind, though, that accreditation of your community college may not be enough for the credits to transfer. Each university may have additional requirements for transfer.

Also, in addition to accreditation of your educational institution, there are also accreditations that are specialized for a specific program. Let's look at examples of these.

Bunker Hill College in Boston, Massachusetts has an entire webpage devoted to accreditations. Note that the first on this page is the institutional accreditation. Additional accreditations listed on this page are specialized. In this case, the specialized programs are primarily in the medical field: registered nursing, medical laboratory technology, surgical technology, etc. (5)

Some community colleges do not have a direct link to accreditation information on its home page. If that's the case, use the search box. Here's an example. Put the word "accreditation" in the Home page search box of Valencia College in Florida and several links appear, including this one that tells you about Valencia's accreditations. (6)

You can also search a database provided by the U.S. Department of Education and titled The Database of Accredited Postsecondary Institutions and Programs. (7) This database is also downloadable as an Excel file.

SEVP Certification

SEVP refers to the **Student and Exchange Visitor Program**. SEVP is a program of U.S. Immigration and Customs Enforcement (ICE) which is a part of the U.S. Department of Homeland Security. According to Homeland Security's website, "SEVP monitors F [academic] and M [vocational] students and their dependents while in the United States to ensure that rules and regulations are followed by international students. The program also certifies schools to allow them to enroll F or M students. International students studying in the United States can only attend an SEVP-certified school. To be certified, schools must prove that they are operational, meaning that they possess the necessary facilities and instructors, and engage in course instruction prior to requesting SEVP certification." (8) Note again what this says:

"International students studying in the United States can only attend an SEVP-certified school."

This means that in addition to making sure your chosen college is academically accredited, the college must also be SEVP-certified. The Department of Homeland Security makes it easy with a webpage designed to search for a specific school and determine if it is certified. (9) You also have the option of downloading the entire list of certified schools.

SEVP also manages **SEVIS**, the **Student and Exchange Visitor Information System**. SEVIS is an on-line system that keeps up-to-date information about SEVP-certified schools, exchange visitor programs certified by the U.S. Department of State, and also F, M, and J [exchange visitors] nonimmigrants, and their dependents. In other words, SEVIS keeps track of the more than 1.2 million F and M visa immigrants to the United States. You are required to be listed in the SEVIS database. To be listed, you will provide a completed I-20 form and pay the I-901 fee. There will be more about this Chapter 4.

Transfer Partnerships

Each community college has **transfer partners**. Some colleges refer to these transfer agreements as "**articulation agreements**." The transfer/articulation partnership tells you that that the community college has developed a special relationship with several four-year colleges and universities to guarantee your course credits will transfer to that institution. By "guaranteed," you must meet the academic requirements of the four-year university. If you meet those requirements, you will achieve automatic acceptance into the partner four-year university.

Community colleges usually develop transfer partnerships with universities in the same state or nearby states. However, some community colleges have developed partnerships with a long list of four-year institutions.

Here are a few examples of transfer relationships within states.

The state of Washington has a Direct Transfer Agreement (DTA) between Washington's community colleges and several four-year universities. The Highline Community College in Des Moines, Washington (just south of Seattle) lists these universities on a separate webpage with details about credit transfers. (10)

Six University of California campuses (Davis, Irvine, Merced, Riverside, Santa Barbara, and Santa Cruz) offer a Transfer Admission Guarantee with California's community colleges. Learn more on the University of California Transfer agreement webpage. (11) There is also an agreement with California State University which has several branches, among them CSU at Chico. (12)

California State University at Chico

Northern Virginia Community College has Guaranteed Admission Agreements with several Virginia universities, among them George Mason University, College of William & Mary, and

Virginia Commonwealth University. (13) In fact, Northern Virginia Community College is part of the Virginia Community College System of 23 community colleges and has extensive guaranteed admission agreements with more than 20 of Virginia's colleges and universities. (14)

Valencia College students in Florida have a guaranteed University Transfer to one of twelve Florida public universities. (15) Bunker Hill Community College in Boston, Massachusetts participates in Mass Transfer (16) and also has articulation agreements in specific academic areas with several Massachusetts higher education institutions. (17) Pima Community College has transfer agreements with the major universities and colleges in Arizona, including the University Arizona in the same city, Tucson. (18)

You can see from these examples that if you have your heart set on studying at a particular four-year college or university, you would be wise to look for a community college that has a transfer partnership with your chosen university. The community college may even be in the same city as your university transfer partner.

When doing your research, look for information on transfer programs on the college's website. If you don't find it, type "transfer" in the search box.

Another way to approach this is to find the four-year university that has a strong academic program in your chosen field. If you know, for example, that you want to study engineering, and if you learn the University of Illinois Urbana-Champaign has a very good engineering school, you will want to look for a community college that has a transfer partnership with Illinois at Urbana-Champaign. Illinois provides an Articulation Guide to help you find those community colleges that have partnerships with the university. (19) Another way to search for a community college that has a transfer agreement with the University of Illinois is to look at the Illinois Articulation Initiative (20) which lists colleges and universities that share a transfer agreement.

Some colleges have a better for transfer rate for students than other colleges do. De Anza College in Cupertino, California transfers 74% of its graduating students each year. According to its website, De Anza boasts "the highest number of students transferring to both University of California (9 campuses, including Berkeley and UCLA) and California State University (23 campuses, including San Jose State and San Francisco State)." (21) Transfer rates refer to all students, not just international students. The factors affecting American students will have an impact on overall transfer rates.

Some four-year colleges accept more transfer students than other colleges. If you are not accepted by your first choice, then try some of the other universities on your list. You may find yourself more welcomed. Again, this refers to all students, not just international students. (22)

Other universities are very competitive, and they only accept a small percentage of new students from all applicants. The University of California at Berkeley (Cal Berkeley) only accepts 8.2% of international students who apply to become first-year (freshmen) students. However, Cal Berkeley admits 24.2% of transfer applicants, and of those, 93% come from a California community college. (23) That is, your chance of being accepted by Cal Berkeley is considerably better if you transfer from a California community college than if you attempt to enter as a freshman or as a transfer from a non-California college. If you have your heart set on studying at Cal Berkeley or Cal Tech or Harvard or Stanford, go ahead and try! But have a backup plan ready.

Tuition and Fees

Unless you are very rich, the cost of an education is always a concern. Generally speaking, private universities are more expensive than public, tax-funded universities. The public universities typically charge an **"in-state"** tuition fee for residents of the home state, and an **"out-of-state"** fee for residents of other states, and international students. Sometimes the out-of-state (also called "**non-resident**" fee) is only a small amount more. More often, the out-of-state/non-resident tuition is considerably more.

In addition to tuition, fees are assessed at the time of registration for classes. Fees cover a range of services available to students. Among the services covered are: health services; library use; entry to athletic events and facilities; use of the campus shuttle bus service; use of the Student Center facilities (restaurants, coffee houses, film programs, meeting rooms, etc.); and technology (computers, databases, and networks). Typically all these services are combined into one fee that you pay along with tuition at the time of registration. The fee is mandatory. Each college has a different set of fees. Some require very few extra fees and other require a larger fee for several services.

You can search for tuition and fees on the website for each college that interests you. Keep in mind that some schools will include estimated cost of living in a total amount for a whole year. Often, these living costs refer to students who stay in college dormitories and eat in the school cafeteria. If you think you can save money by sharing an apartment with other students and cooking your own meals, then your overall costs for a year will be lower. Read carefully to see if a quoted one-year amount includes the cost of housing and meals to get an accurate idea of how much you'll have to pay.

U.S. News has a good directory of U.S. community colleges with information about tuition and fees. (24) Let's take a look at a couple of listings. Go to http://www.usnews.com/education/community-colleges and click on "Virginia." Scroll down to "Northern Virginia Community College." Over on your right, you see that students at Northern Virginia (NOVA) pay $3,677 for in-state tuition and fees, and $8,411 for out-of-state tuition and fees. These out-of-state tuition and fees apply to international students. Check the college website to get the most recent data. Also this directory is not complete because not every community college is listed. Go to your selected college website for more information.

How about Santa Barbara City College in Santa Barbara, California? Using the same website, we find in-state tuition and fees are $1,374, and out-of-state are $7,254. CUNY Kingsborough Community College in New York City has tuition and fees of $1,374 (in-state) and $7,254 (out-of-state). Pima Community College in Tucson, Arizona, has in-state tuition and fees of $1,724 and $8,048 for out-of-state and international students. Again, check the college website for the latest figures.

Most financial aid that is available to American students is not available to international students. International students can borrow money from an American bank, but the student must have an American citizen or permanent resident as a loan **cosigner**. This means the cosigner agrees to be responsible for repaying the loan if you do not repay it. (25)

Relatively few American colleges and universities provide outright financial aid and scholarships to international students. Search this database to see which schools do provide aid (26). Be sure to ask your college advisor about the availability of any funds for international students. Two additional sources of information about funding for international students studying at community colleges are Education USA, published by the U.S. State Department (27), and the Institute of International Education. (28)

Also keep in mind that cost-of-living varies widely in different American cities. It may be worth it to pay a little more for tuition and fees if the cost-of-living is significantly lower. We'll look at cost-of-living in the next section.

Community-College Location:
Cost of Living, Transportation, Climate, Culture

Cost of living

Not all international students want to live in an on-campus **dormitory,** which is housing and meals provided for a fee by the

college. **Homestays** are one option. In a homestay, you rent a
room for a fee in the home of a local resident. Meals may or may
not be included. Be sure to ask if you get **room and board** (meals)
or only a room.

However, most international students prefer to rent an
apartment, and live off-campus. Cost-of-living for an apartment
includes the monthly rental fee, often plus utilities (gas, electricity,
water), as well as food, clothing, household items, etc. Rent will
likely be the most expensive item.

The cost-of-living varies widely from city to city in the United
States. It is generally true that small cities and rural areas have
lower costs than large urban areas. Cities in the American South
and Southwest tend to be less expensive than northern, East Coast,
and West Coast cities.

Let's look at the average cost of renting a one-bedroom
apartment in select American cities, all with a community college
profiled in this book. This information comes from the website
Numbeo (29), a website that gives average costs in various cities
for rents, food, transportation and more.

One-bedroom apartment rent for one month (data is from
early 2016), with lower costs outside the city center and higher
costs in the city center:

Austin, TX: $978 to $1,530
Boston, MA: $1,570 to $2,296
Chicago, IL: $1,026 to $1,557
New York, NY: $ 1,810 to $ 2,971
Orlando, FL: $ 878 to $1, 230
Reston, VA: $ 1,460 to $ 1,777.50
Santa Barbara, CA: $ 1,338 to 1,802
Seattle, WA: $1,267 to $1,714
Tucson, AZ: $525 to $598
Washington, DC: $1,585 to $2,028

Keep this in mind. If you choose an apartment outside the
city center because it costs less, you'll have higher transportation

costs to travel to the college campus. If you live near the campus, you may be able to walk or ride a bicycle and save on transportation costs.

There are other considerations as well. Do you want to live in a small, quiet town or a huge, busy city? A smaller town usually has more opportunities for meeting local people, and usually a lower crime rate, too. Some of the smaller towns are near some of America's great national parks. Or perhaps you have an interest such as snow skiing. You might prefer living in a small town near a ski resort.

Students at Colorado Mountain College

Larger cities have many more cultural opportunities and more extensive transportation systems. Your chances of finding food from your home country will be better in a large city because of immigrants who have opened restaurants and grocery stores devoted to Chinese, Thai, Ethiopian, Brazilian food, etc. However, the cost-of-living is higher as are crime rates.

Do you want to have easy access to airports that will take you home and back again? Transportation costs also include airfare to and from the United States. If you fly to east Asia or southeast Asia, choosing a college near one of the large West Coast international airports (Los Angeles, San Francisco, Seattle) means you will pay less to fly home. If you are coming from Latin America, a city such as Tucson, Phoenix, Austin, Miami, or Orlando will provide cheaper flights. Some flights go over the North Pole so flying out of Chicago may be less expensive.

What about climate? Do you like four seasons or do you prefer to live in a place that is warm most of the year? If you love snow skiing, then go to the mountains of Colorado or Vermont. If you like sunny, warm weather, then perhaps Orlando, Tucson, and Austin are your best choices. Of course, you don't choose a college just because of weather. But if you have more than one good option to choose from, weather may be a factor that helps you decide.

What about culture? Do you want to live in a location that has lots of cultural opportunities (festivals, art exhibits, music, etc.) or a place that has great sporting events (football, basketball) or opportunities for individual sports (bicycling, skiing, hiking, surfing)?

You'll spend several years living in the United States. What kind of experience do you want to have?

Common Mistakes Made by International Students

Not doing your research and not planning ahead!
This chapter shows beyond a doubt that knowing as much as you can possibly know in advance is going to help you make the best decisions. Do your research and plan ahead. Know what professional career you want to enter. Know where you want to go

to undergraduate and possibly graduate school. Know where you want to go to community college to study.

Not asking questions

Colleges have people on the staff who get paid to answer questions. Don't be shy! Ask questions about the college, its admission requirements, and its transfer programs. If you can't find the information you need on the college website, email and ask someone.

Not putting yourself forward

This is not a time to be shy about your achievements. If you've made really excellent scores on exams, then be sure that your college knows this. Being too modest can hurt you.

Not improving your English-listening comprehension

You may read and write English quite well, but still you have problems speaking with native speakers and understanding them when they speak. Before you leave your home country, take as many opportunities as possible to speak to native English speakers, especially those from the U.S. and Canada (similar accents). Ask the native speaker to describe life in the U.S. and to give advice on how to be a successful student in the U.S.

Let's Put it All Together

Let's imagine that you've done a lot of thinking about your future. You've chosen a career, and you've outlined a path to employment in that profession. You want to save money, and you want to improve your English before going on to the four-year university. You've decided to begin your studies at an American community college instead of a four-year university. So let's take a few examples to see how you might choose a specific four-year university and a specific community college.

This section refers to these two websites to get rankings of four-year and graduate-level universities.
U.S. News. Best Global Universities (30)
Best College Rankings and Lists (31)

Engineering: You want to study engineering, but you haven't decided yet which subfield of engineering is right for you so you look for four-year bachelor's general engineering programs. You found that the University of Illinois at Urbana-Champaign is number five in the list of best undergraduate general engineering programs. The University of Illinois is part of the Illinois Articulation Initiative. (32) Check out the profiles for Harper College and Kaskaskia College in Illinois, which may be good choices for you. Both of these community colleges participate in the Illinois Articulation Initiative, and both have transfer agreements with the University of Illinois. Note also that the University of Michigan is #6 on this list of best engineering programs, Cornell University is #9, and the University of Texas at Austin is #11. The universities all have transfer partnerships with community colleges in their states and elsewhere.

Business/Economics/Accounting: You see an opportunity to open your own accounting firm in your homeland, and perhaps teach accounting at a local university. You search for a great accounting program in the United States and find the University of Texas at Austin is ranked #1 in accounting. The University of Illinois at Urbana-Champaign is #2. Consider Austin Community College which has a transfer partnership with the University of Texas at Austin. (33) You have already looked at transfer partnerships with Illinois through the Illinois Articulation Initiative.

Environmental Science: No doubt, the environment is a growing concern in countries around the world. You see an opportunity for a career in this field. The University of California at Davis has an environment/ecology program that is ranked #3 globally. UC

Davis participates in the TAG (Transfer Admission Guarantee) program with California community colleges. (34)

Space Science/Astronomy: Has your government declared an interest in astronomy and space exploration? You have an interest in working in this profession. You find that the University of California at Santa Cruz is #4 in this field, and the University of Arizona at Tucson is #6. You already know about the California TAG program. The University of Arizona has a transfer agreement with Pima Community College for the study of astronomy. (35) Both Pima CC and the University of Arizona are in the city of Tucson.

Tourism and Hospitality Industry: Is your home country interested in building the tourism industry? You are considering a career in the tourism and hospitality industry because you see an opportunity there. You find that Cornell University has the #1 program in the School of Hotel Administration. Cornell has articulation agreements (transfer partnerships) with several colleges. (36) CUNY Kingsborough Community College in Brooklyn, New York, is one of those colleges. (37)

~~~

In the next chapter, we'll discuss how students go about applying for admission to community colleges around the United States.

Footnotes and Links: Chapter 2

(1) Best College Rankings and Lists, *U.S. News.*
http://colleges.usnews.rankingsandreviews.com/best-colleges/rankings
(2) Valencia College film program.
http://catalog.valenciacollege.edu/degrees/associateinscience/arts entertainment/filmproductiontechnology/

(3) Community Colleges, *US News*.
http://www.usnews.com/education/community-colleges
(4) FAQs About Accreditation. U.S. Department of Education.
http://ope.ed.gov/accreditation/FAQAccr.aspx
(5) Bunker Hill Community College accreditations.
http://www.bhcc.mass.edu/academics/accreditation/
(6) Valencia College accreditations
http://catalog.valenciacollege.edu/
(7) U.S. Department of Education, The Database of Accredited
Postsecondary Institutions and Programs
http://ope.ed.gov/accreditation/
(8) Student and Exchange Visitor Program (SEVP). Who Is SEVP?
https://studyinthestates.dhs.gov/2015/01/who-is-sevp
(9) Search for SEVP schools.
https://studyinthestates.dhs.gov/school-search
(10) Highline Community College, Direct Transfer Agreement.
https://transfercenter.highline.edu/DTASchoolsl.php
(11) University of California Transfer Admission Guarantee
http://admission.universityofcalifornia.edu/transfer/guarantee/
(12) The California State University. CSU Student Transfer.
http://calstate.edu/transfer/degrees/
(13) Northern Virginia Community College. Guaranteed
Admission Agreements. http://www.nvcc.edu/gaa/
(14) Virginia Community College System. Guaranteed Transfer
http://www.vccs.edu/students/transfers/
(15) Valencia College. University Transfer.
http://international.valenciacollege.edu/academics/university-transfer/
(16) Bunker Hill Community College, Mass Transfer.
http://www.bhcc.mass.edu/transfer/transferprograms/
(17) Bunker Hill Community College. Articulation Agreements.
http://www.bhcc.mass.edu/admissions/articulationagreements/
(18) Pima Community College, Transfer Partnerships.
https://www.pima.edu/current-students/transferring-from-pima/transfer-partnerships.html

(19) University of Illinois Urbana-Champaign. Articulation Guide. https://admissions.illinois.edu/Apply/Transfer/TransferArticulati onGuide

(20) Illinois Articulation Initiative. http://www.itransfer.org/IAI/participating.aspx?section=students

(21) De Anza College. https://www.deanza.edu/international/transfer.html

(22) US News. Most Transfer Students. http://colleges.usnews.rankingsandreviews.com/best-colleges/rankings/most-transfers

(23) University of California at Berkeley. Transfer Admission. http://admissions.berkeley.edu/studentprofile http://admission.universityofcalifornia.edu/campuses/berkeley/tr ansfer-profile/

(24) US News. Community Colleges. http://www.usnews.com/education/community-colleges

(25) InternationalStudentLoans.com http://www.internationalstudentloan.com/international_student/

(26) InternationalStudent.com Schools Awarding Financial Aid. http://www.internationalstudent.com/schools_awarding_aid/

(27) Education USA. Community College. https://educationusa.state.gov/your-5-steps-us-study/finance-your-studies/community-college

(28) Institute of International Education. Funding for U.S. Study. http://www.fundingusstudy.org/

(29) Numbeo. Cost-of-Living. http://www.numbeo.com/cost-of-living/

(30) U.S. News. Best Global Universities. http://www.usnews.com/education/best-global-universities

(31) U.S. News. Best College Rankings and Lists. http://colleges.usnews.rankingsandreviews.com/best-colleges/rankings?int=a8f209

(32) University of Illinois Urbana-Champaign. Articulation Guide. https://admissions.illinois.edu/Apply/Transfer/TransferArticulati onGuide and

Illinois Articulation Initiative.
http://www.itransfer.org/IAI/participating.aspx?section=students
(33) Austin Community College, University Transfer and
Equivalency Guides. http://www.austincc.edu/degrees-and-
certificates/earn-a-degree-and-transfer/prepare-for-transfer/us-
university-transfer-and-equivalency-guides
(34) University of California at Davis. Transfer Admission
Guarantee.
https://www.ucdavis.edu/admissions/undergraduate/transfer/pla
nning http://tag.ucdavis.edu/
(35) University of Arizona. Pima Pathway Agreements. Astronomy.
https://admissions.arizona.edu/transfer/pima-pathways-
agreements
(36) Cornell University. A Guide for Transfer Students.
http://admissions.cornell.edu/sites/admissions.cornell.edu/files/T
ransfer%20Guide%202013-14.pdf
    (37) Kingsborough Community College. Tourism and
Hospitality.
http://www.kbcc.cuny.edu/academicdepartments/tah/Pages/defa
ult.aspx

Chapter 3. Applying to a Community College

The steps for applying for admission to a community college are:

- fill out an application form;
- pay the application fee to the college;
- submit additional required documentation with your application form, including proof of financial support, transcripts, etc.;
- submit TOEFL, IELTS, iTEP, Pearson Academic, or Eiken (Japanese) scores.

These steps describe the basic process. But we know from the previous Chapter 2 that you must do a considerable amount of work before you begin the application process. You can apply to more than one college if you wish.

First, you must determine that each college which interests you is SEVP-certified and regionally academically-accredited. There is no point in applying to a college that is not SEVP-certified. Schools that are not SEVP certified may not accept international students. Furthermore, your course credits will not be transferable to a four-year university if the school is not academically accredited.

Second, do your research and become very familiar with each college you are considering. Study the college website. Don't be afraid to ask questions of the college staff. There will be a **Designated School Official (DSO)** at your college who will be able to answer your questions. Does the college meet your academic and career goals? Is the college affordable? Is the college located in a place that you can afford to live? Is any financial aid available? Does the college have a transfer partnership with a four-year university where you would like to transfer to earn your bachelor's degree? What kind of assistance does the college provide for international students? Are there any opportunities at the community college to study and improve your English?

Key Fact: There is no central admission process for all American community colleges. Each college has its own admission process. You must study the college website to learn the details of your college's application process. Look under the terms "Admissions."

Admission Deadlines and Fees

Most colleges have application deadlines for each term though the actual dates differ from college to college. For example, Valencia College in Orlando, Florida, has an application deadline of June 15, 2016, for the fall of 2016. (1) Note that international students must apply earlier than those living in the U.S., and they must supply all required documents when they apply, not just the application form.

Approximately 200 American colleges have "**rolling admissions**," which means that the college will accept your application within an extended time period such as six months. Some community colleges have scheduled application deadlines for admission for most programs, but they may also have rolling admissions for specific programs within the college. Bunker Hill Community College is an example of this. Bunker Hill's Allied Health Program has rolling admissions (2), but general admission to other Bunker Hill programs has a deadline of July 15 for the fall semester, and November 30 for spring semester. (3)

Many colleges in the U.S., both community colleges and four-year colleges, follow a semester schedule. That is, there are classes in a fall semester, in a spring semester, and also summer classes. Other schools have a quarter schedule with a fall, winter, and spring quarters. Summers are set aside for intensive courses in English and other classes. De Anza College follows the quarter schedule and has deadlines of June 30 for the fall quarter, October 31 for winter, and January 31 for the spring quarter. (4)

Some colleges allow you to fill out an application form on-line; other colleges do not allow on-line applications. Instead, the college provides a paper form, which you fill out, and then return by mail or by email as an attached PDF file. Here is an application form for Santa Barbara City College. (5) Note the application deadlines are on this form.

You must pay an application fee to the college at the time you send your application form requesting admission. The application fee is a different amount at each college. Methods of paying the fee include money order, check, or credit card. Some schools accept wire transfers of money from your home country bank. Santa Monica College in Santa Monica, California, is an example of this wire transfer method. (6)

Each college will have its own application requirements, although there are many documents that all colleges will require. Read the college website carefully.

Early Decision and Early Action

Early decision is a phrase indicating that you apply early and you agree to enroll if your college accepts your application. Early decision applications are legally binding. If accepted, you must attend that college. Note that many community colleges do not offer these early decision and early action options.

It is crucial for you to remember that if you apply for early decision, be very, very certain that the college is your first choice. You are legally required to attend the college if you accept early decision. You must be certain the college is your first choice.

Early action indicates that you applied early and were accepted early, but you have some time to decide whether you will accept or not. You have until the normal decision date, usually May 1. Early action programs are not legally binding.

There are advantages and disadvantages to early decision so know more about this before you agree. A good commentary explaining early decision and early action plus the positives and negatives is found on the College Board website (7).

Another discussion on early decision and early action for international students is found at Unigo.com. There we see the same warnings for international students. Early decision is not always the best decision for you.

Proof of Sufficient Funding

At the time you apply, you will be required to provide proof that you can pay for your expenses during the time you are living in the United States. Expenses include a) tuition and fees; b) living expenses, including books, supplies, rent, food, etc.; and c) health insurance.

Your college will provide information about estimated costs for tuition and fees and living expenses. Most colleges also provide a student health insurance program which you can purchase. In Chapter 7, Living in the U.S., we'll go into more detail about the U.S. health care system, with information on expenses that are not covered by your health insurance.

On your financial statement, you have options of: a) providing proof you have sufficient funds in a U.S. bank to cover your expenses; b) providing proof that you have a parent or other family member with savings to cover your expenses; c) providing proof you have an American sponsor who will cover your expenses; d) you have a government scholarship sufficient for expected expenses, or e) you have another source of funds that will cover your expenses.

Typically, to prove that you are in "good standing" and have sufficient funds to study in the U.S., you must provide a letter from your U.S. bank and a notarized bank statement showing a balance of how much is in your account. Some colleges use a form provided by the U.S. Citizenship and Immigration Services called the Affidavit of Support Form I-134. (8) Other colleges have their own forms to use.

Your college will provide specifics of this required information, and often will provide the actual forms you must fill out and provide to the college. See Footnote/Link (9) for some actual forms provided by community colleges that give more information about the financial statement required. Look over these forms to see the kind of information required. Then go to the website of your chosen college and look for information. Terms vary. Look for terms like *Financial Statement, Financial Certificate, Declaration of Finances, Affidavit of Support.* Typically there are links on the International Students Admissions page to these required forms.

Each college has its own procedures for providing this financial information. Ask your designated school officer (DSO) which form your college requires.

Additional Funding

International students don't have the student financial aid available to them that is available to American citizens. International students must rely primarily on their own savings or their parents' savings. However, there are scholarships available for international students.

At the time that you apply for admission to your community college, be sure to ask the DSO at your college's advising center about scholarships available to international students. Another good source of information is your home government. Your home government may provide scholarships for study in a particular academic area.

InternationalStudent.com has a good database of scholarships available to international students. You search this site by a) the field you want to study, for example, engineering; b) your country of origin; and c) the country where you will be studying – in this case, the U.S.A. You can read the descriptions of available scholarships. To get full contact information for each scholarship, register for the International Student website at InternationalStudent.com. (10)

Additional good sources of information about available scholarships and loans for international students are:

- International Education Financial Aid at IEFA.org; (11)
- InternationalScholarships.com; (12)
- InternationalStudentLoan.com (13)

Other Documents and Forms

I-20 Form

The **I-20 form** is the "**Certificate of Eligibility** for Nonimmigrant (F-1) Student Status – For Academic and Language Students." Note that this refers to the F-1 visa that is the visa for most students. Form I-20 is required by the U.S. Department of Homeland Security. You must fill out and submit this form in order to get a visa to study in the United States. Usually your college will provide this form. Some community colleges require that you submit an I-20 form at the same time that you submit your application form. More often, though, you will be asked to submit the I-20 form after your college has accepted you as a student. We will discuss the I-20 and other required forms and fees in Chapter 4 on visas and forms.

Transcripts

You will also be asked to provide copies of your official **transcripts** from high school and from any intensive English course you may have taken. You must provide transcripts in your native language and English translations of the transcripts.

Letters of Recommendation

Letters of recommendation from two of your high school teachers are not always required, but they are helpful to submit with your application. If your college officials know more about you, they are more likely to accept you as a student. These letters should also be translated into English

Your teachers are your best source of recommendation letters. Make appointments with two teachers. Ask each of them to write a one-page letter of recommendation. Chat with your teacher and let him/her know about your academic achievements.

Also tell your teacher about activities you've been involved in. Examples are playing on the school soccer team, playing a musical instrument in the school orchestra, participating in a neighborhood clean-up program, or participating in a children's after-school program. The teacher can add this information to the letter.

Why do you want to include this information? American college officials look at more than just your academic work. They want to see your **extracurricular activities**, to see that you are a well-rounded student who has made a contribution to your school and your community.

Passport Photo and Immunization Proof

Many colleges require a copy of the interior page of your passport showing your photo. You may also be asked for an additional photo of yourself.

Also required by most colleges is proof that you have been vaccinated for measles, mumps, and rubella and other infectious diseases. Some colleges require this proof at the time you apply for admission. Other colleges will ask for you to show this to your DSO (designated school official) when you arrive at your college.

Examples of Required Forms and Documents

Here are some examples of the forms and documents required by three community colleges - Santa Barbara City College, CUNY Kingsborough in New York City, and Western Wyoming Community College. (14) Before you apply, read the submission requirements carefully. Have all required documents ready.

Proving Your English-Language Proficiency

American community colleges will expect you to prove that you speak, read, and write English well enough to be a successful student. If you come from a country where English is the common language, then you can get a waiver and you will not be required to take a proficiency test. An example of this is Valencia College in Florida. The college provides a list of English-speaking countries. (15) If you are from one of these countries, you will not be required to prove English-language proficiency.

There are several tests you can take to demonstrate your English-language proficiency. The most commonly used is the **TOEFL** (Test of English as a Foreign Language). Others are **IELTS** (International English Language Testing System), iTEP (International Test of English Proficiency), PTE Academic (Pearson), or EIKEN Test in Practical English Proficiency (STEP Eiken).

The TOEFL test has three forms with three possible scores: **iBT** (internet-based test), **CBT** (computer-based test), or **PBT** (paper-based test). Each college has its own minimum score requirements. Community college websites provide specific information about which test the college requires and what the minimum required score must be to register for academic programs.

An **academic program** in this context means that your English is sufficient to succeed in regular academic classes at the college. These academic class credits can be transferred later to a four-year university to count toward your bachelor's degree. Look carefully and find the minimum scores for your chosen college to be allowed to enroll in academic classes.

For example, Austin Community College in Austin, Texas, provides detailed information on its website about the testing options and scores required. (16) Austin CC requires "TOEFL scores of 530 (paper-based test) or 71 (Internet-based test) with a 53 composite score in reading, listening, and writing sections." Mesa Community College in Mesa, Arizona (Phoenix metro area), requires 61 iBT, 173 CBT, or 500 PBT. (17) Highline College, Des Moines, Washington (Seattle area), requires 480 on the written test (PBT) or 54 on the iBT. (18)

There are some colleges such as Shoreline Community College, Shoreline, Washington (Seattle area), and Santa Barbara College in Santa Barbara, California, that do not require a TOEFL test score for admission, although they will accept the TOEFL score if you took the TOEFL test. Students at these colleges are given an assessment test upon arrival, and the students are placed at the appropriate class level.

Actually, **assessment tests** (also called **placement tests**) for all students, not just international students, are very common at all community colleges. If your assessment test score for English is not sufficiently high, you will be required to enroll in **ESL (English as a Second Language)** classes first. Later, as your English improves, you will be allowed to enroll in the academic classes. If you are required to take ESL courses before you can enroll in academic courses, your time at the community college will be extended. We go into more detail about the assessment tests in Chapter 6.

Many community colleges offer **conditional admission**. This means that you may be admitted to the college on a conditional basis. You will be required to finish certain courses to improve your English proficiency.

Many students take TOEFL-preparation classes or even hire a personal tutor. There are many websites with information about preparing for the TOEFL. Keep in mind also that the same advice you will get for taking any test also applies to the TOEFL and other English-language proficiency tests. Put in some study time every day. Don't try to learn everything on the night before the test. Practice speaking with native English speakers, listen to English-language radio, television, and films. Read news in English. The internet offers plenty of interesting things to read in English. Most important of all, get enough sleep on the night before you take the test. Research has indicated with a well-rested student does better on a test than an exhausted student.

Do Your Research!

As we saw in the last Chapter 2, Choosing a College, we again see in this chapter on college application and admission how important it is to learn as much as possible before you apply. The more you know, the easier the process will be. You don't want any huge last-minute surprises that delay your plans to study at an American community college.

EducationUSA is an excellent source of information for international students who are ready to apply for submission to an American community college. This organization is sponsored by the U.S. State Department. EducationUSA has more than 400 advising centers all over the world where you can find information about applying for admission to an American college. You can speak to an adviser directly. Information and advising are free of charge. Go to EducationUSA's website for a list of advising centers. (19)

In the next chapter, we'll start with the assumption that you've been accepted into the college of your choice. You have agreed to become a student at the college. Now it is time to get a visa to study in the U.S.A.

Footnotes and Links: Chapter 3

(1) Valencia College. Application Deadlines.
http://international.valenciacollege.edu/admissions/application-deadlines/
(2) Bunker Hill Community College. Allied Health Application.
http://www.bhcc.mass.edu/alliedhealth/applicationprocess/
(3) Bunker Hill Community College. International Students. Guide to Admissions.
http://www.bhcc.mass.edu/internationalcenter/guidetoadmissions/
(4) De Anza College. International Students. Admission.
https://www.deanza.edu/international/admission.html#deadline
(5) Santa Barbara City College. International Student Admission Application.
http://international.sbcc.edu/apply/forms/pdf/00%20Int%20Application.pdf
(6) Santa Monica College. International Student Tuition and Fees.
https://www.smc.edu/EnrollmentDevelopment/IEC/Pages/Tuition_Fees.aspx
(7) College Board. Early Decision & Early Action.
https://professionals.collegeboard.com/guidance/applications/early
(8) U.S. Department of Citizenship and Immigration Services.
Forms. https://www.uscis.gov/forms
(9) Financial Affidavit Forms: Kaskaskia College, Centralia, IL.
International Financial Certificate.
http://www.kaskaskia.edu/PDFs/ProspectiveStudents/InternationalFinancialCertificate.pdf

Santa Monica College, Santa Monica, CA
https://www.smc.edu/EnrollmentDevelopment/IEC/Documents/Admissions_and_Enrollment_Forms/Financial_Statement.pdf
Pima Community College, Tucson, AZ
https://www.pima.edu/new-students/international/docs/Affidavit_of_Support.pdf
Valencia College. Declaration of Finances, 2015 (and other forms).
http://international.valenciacollege.edu/admissions/admissions-forms/
(10) International Student. International Student & Study Abroad Scholarship Search.
http://www.internationalstudent.com/scholarships/
(11) International Education Financial Aid. International Financial Aid and College Scholarship Search. http://www.iefa.org/
(12) InternationalScholarships.com
http://www.internationalscholarships.com/
(13) InternationalStudentLoan.com
http://www.internationalstudentloan.com/
(14) Examples of Required Supporting Documents:
Santa Barbara City College,
http://international.sbcc.edu/apply/checklist/
CUNY Kingsborough Community College
http://www.kbcc.cuny.edu/sub-apply_now/Pages/international_freshman_app_require.aspx
Western Wyoming Community College. Steps to Enrollment.
https://www.westernwyoming.edu/admissions/international/requirements.html
(15) Valencia College. List of English speaking Countries and Territories.
http://international.valenciacollege.edu/downloads/Valencia-List-of-English-Speaking-Countries.pdf
(16) Austin Community College, English Proficiency Requirement.

AMERICAN COMMUNITY COLLEGES

http://www.austincc.edu/apply-and-register/type-of-student/international-admission-steps/english-proficiency-requirement

(17) Mesa Community College, The Admissions Process Requirement. https://www.mesacc.edu/international-education/future-f-1-students/transfer-f-1-students

(18) Highline College, How to Apply. https://international.highline.edu/admissions/howToApply.htm

(19) EducationUSA.com. Find an Advising Center. https://educationusa.state.gov/find-advising-center

Chapter 4 – Visas and Forms

In this chapter, we learn about the I-20 form which will be provided to you by your community college, and the I-901 form and fee you must pay for your required listing in the SERVIS database. We'll discuss visas and how to acquire one for travel to the U.S. Keep in mind that regulations can change so be sure to check linked websites for current information.

Forms I-20 and I-901

As mentioned in earlier chapters, the **Student and Exchange Visitor Program (SEVP)** is a part of U.S. Immigration and Customs Enforcement (ICE). The SEVP program "helps DHS (Department of Homeland Security) and the Department of State monitor school and exchange visitor programs, nonimmigrant students and exchange visitors and their dependents." (1) This monitoring function includes all international students on F1 visas.

According to Homeland Security's website, SEVP monitors F (academic) and M (vocational) visa students and their dependents while in the United States "to ensure that rules and regulations are followed by international students. The program also certifies schools to enroll F or M students. International students studying in the United States can only attend an SEVP-certified school." (2)

The designated school official (DSO) at your chosen community college will provide you with the I-20 form. At many colleges, the form will come to you after you've been accepted into the college. At other colleges, you will be required to submit the I-20 form at the same time as you submit your application for admission form.

Note that there is a date on your I-20 form. You must apply for a U.S. visa within 120 days before the date on the I-20 form. The I-20 form is for either the F or the M visa. Make sure your I-20 form is for the visa you need to study in the U.S. Keep the completed I-20 form in a safe place. You will likely be required to show it to Immigration & Customs Enforcement when you enter the U.S. You will also need it to get a **driver's license** and a **Social Security number**. The I-20 proves that you are officially enrolled in a SEVP-certified college. You can find more information about the I-20 form and the I-901 form on the Study in the States website. (3)

Important reminder: If you leave the U.S. temporarily while studying here - for example, to visit your family in your home country - you must maintain your I-20 status at your school. To do this, you may not leave the U.S. for more than five months, and your I-20 must be valid for at least one semester after you return. Talk to your designated school officer (DSO) and ask what you must do to maintain your I-20. Your college must be informed of your travel plans.

SEVP manages **SEVIS, the Student and Exchange Visitor Information System**, an internet-based system that contains information on international students and their schools. It is also used by SEVP to help monitor students and schools for compliance with U.S. law.

To be listed in the SEVIS database, you must provide a completed I-20 form and pay the fee attached to form I-901. (4) You cannot get a visa until you've paid your I-901 fee. So be sure to get a receipt to prove that you've made the payment.

Applying for a Visa

A visa is a travel document issued by the nation that you plan to visit, in this case the United States. Visas are placed in the traveler's passport and will be shown to immigration officials upon entering the U.S. There are two basic categories of visas:

nonimmigrant and immigrant. The nonimmigrant visa is for individuals who plan to travel to the U.S. on a temporary basis. This includes students who plan to study in the U.S. Immigrant visas are for those persons who plan to live permanently in the U.S. (5) There are three types of student visas: F, J, and M. (6) We will concern ourselves primarily with the F1 visa for academic studies.

Steps for Applying for a Visa

complete an on-line visa application by filling out form DS-160;

provide a photo with your DS-160 application;
schedule an interview;
pay fees;
collect together all required documents;
prepare for the interview;
attend the interview.

The U.S. State Department's Travel website provides an overview of the visa application process. (7) In addition to the information on this website, you also must contact the U.S. Embassy or Consulate in your home country for information specific to your home country and to schedule an interview. Don't forget that you are required to apply for a U.S. visa within 120 days of the date on the I-20 form you received.

Form DS-160 and Your Photo

Form **DS-160** is the online method of applying for a visa. Find the application form (DS-160) on the Consular Electronic Application Center website (U.S. State Department – Apply for a Nonimmigrant Visa page), fill it out online, and then submit it online. (8)

You may have questions about this application process. If so, check the FAQ (frequently asked questions) page (9) that gives you information on what documents you need, how to answer questions, and how to upload a photo of yourself.

More information about the requirements for the photo that must accompany your visa application is on the State Department's Photo Requirements page. (10)

Note that you are required to take your confirmation page for the DS-160 application form with you when you go for an interview at the U.S. Embassy or Consulate. Be sure to print the confirmation page and keep it in a safe place. You also will be required to take two identical, printed photos of yourself to your visa interview.

Schedule an Interview

Your next step is to schedule an interview at a U.S. Embassy or Consulate in your home country.

Do you know where the nearest U.S. Embassy or Consulate is? That is your first step – find an embassy or consulate to visit. The United States government makes this easy for you in a website entitled USEmbassy.gov. (11) On the map provided, let's look first at the Western Hemisphere. There you will find links to U.S. embassies, consulates, and diplomatic missions from Argentina to Venezuela.

There are always wait times for getting a visa interview and for processing your interview. The wait times depend on the specific U.S. Embassy or Consulate in your country. Plan ahead so that you have enough time for the visa interview and processing and still arrive in the U.S. on time to begin your classes. The U.S. State Department provides you a box to type in the city where your Embassy/Consulate is located to get an estimate of how long the wait time will be. (12) Here are some examples of wait times for different cities around the world: Mexico City – 1 day; Asunción, Paraguay – 4 days; Chengdu, PR China – 2 days; Ho Chi Minh City, Vietnam – 4 days; Nairobi, Kenya – 14 days; Stockholm, Sweden – 2 days; Kolkata, India – 4 days; Riyadh, Saudi Arabia – 3 days.

Pay Fees

At the present time, the fee to apply for a visa is $160.00. Note that this is the fee to *apply* for a visa. There is a separate fee for the visa itself that is called the "visa issuance" fee. Citizens of some countries do not have to pay this fee. For those who must pay, the visa issuance fee varies from country to country. The U.S. Embassy or Consulate in your home country will have instructions on paying this fee. For an estimate of how much the fee will be, go to the U.S. State Department's Visitor Visa website (13), scroll down to Prepare for Your Interview and put your home country in the box titled "Select your nationality to see Issuance Fee." You will then have to select the type of visa you need, which is F1 for students.

Collect Together Your Required Documents

In preparation for your visa interview, gather these documents: your passport, your DS-160 confirmation page, the receipt for your application fee payment. Some countries' U.S. Embassy or Consulate also required a photo of you. This is in addition to the photos you uploaded with your DS-160 visa application form. Make sure your passport is good for the next six months and will not expire during that time period.

Be sure to check with your home country's U.S. Embassy or Consulate to see if any additional documents are required. You may be asked for financial information about how you intend to pay for your education, your academic records (transcripts, diplomas, standardized test scores).

Prepare for Your Visa Interview

Here are some topics to consider for your interview:

Proofread your documents in advance. Be certain that your name and birthdate are correct and the same on all documents. If there is an error, have it corrected by the agency that issued it.

Take all needed documents with you to the interview.

Be prepared to explain what you plan to do for work in your home country after you complete your American education. Make it clear that your intention is to return home and not to immigrate permanently to the U.S.

Check Your Visa and Receive Your Sealed Documents

When your visa has been issued and placed in your passport, be sure to check that everything is correct. If there are errors, return the passport with visa and ask for corrections.

The officer at the U.S. Embassy or Consulate will give you all your immigration papers in a sealed envelope and attach it to your passport. Do not open this envelope. The envelope will opened by Customs and Border Protection agents when you arrive in the U.S.

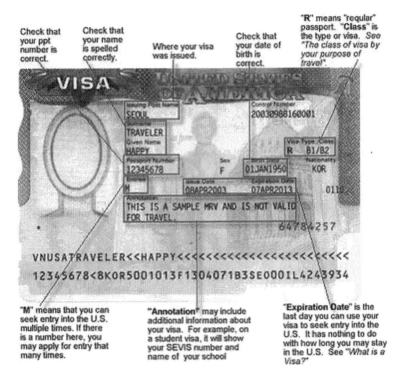

Sample U.S. Visa

What If Your Visa Is Denied?

Most visa applications are approved. Those that are not approved are denied based on reasons established in U.S. law. According to the U.S. State Department's Travel pages on visas, the reasons that visa applications are denied are "because the consular officer does not have all of the information required to determine if the applicant is eligible to receive a visa, because the applicant does not qualify for the visa category for which he or she applied, or because the information reviewed indicates the applicant falls within the scope of one of the inadmissibility or ineligibility grounds of the law. An applicant's current and/or past actions, such as drug or criminal activities, as examples, may make the applicant ineligible for a visa." (14)

There was an interesting article on the website of the Consulate General of the United States, Shanghai, China, in 2000. The head of visa operations at the U.S. Embassy in China, Consul General David Hopper, met with Chinese students to talk about the "secrets" to getting a visa approved. (15) Key points are that you must be able to prove that you are actually a student, and that you are going to the U.S. to study, not work. You must prove that you have enough money to cover the cost of your studies and living expenses. Come to your interview prepared, and with all your documentation. Answer interview questions sincerely. Indicate that you intend to maintain ties to your homeland and your family. Listen carefully to the official if your visa is denied so you will fully understand why. Then you will be able to correct the problem in the future.

Yes, you can try again later if your visa is denied. But you will have to pay the visa application fee again. It is not refundable.

Maintaining Your Visa Status

It will be your responsibility to maintain your F-1 visa while studying in the U.S. This involves making sure your passport has not expired, extending your I-20 form if needed, enrolling full-time as a student, etc. InternationalStudent.com has detailed information about the things you must do to maintain your legal status as a international student in the U.S. (16)

Visa Waiver Program

The United States has an agreement with several countries that make it possible to waive the normal visa acquisition procedures for specific types of travel. Students do not qualify for the Visa Waiver program. See more information about this on the Student Visa page of the U.S. State Department's Travel website. (17).

Before Your Flight

Assuming all goes well and your visa is approved, it's time to start making travel plans. We'll go into more detail about entering the U.S. in the next chapter.

Inform your college of your arrival date. Investigate and arrange for housing upon arrival and transportation to your college.

Gather together any medications you will need as well as prescriptions from your doctor. Also get a copy of your prescription for eye glasses.

If you plan to drive a car in the U.S., be sure to bring your international driver's license from your home country. If you do not have one, take time to get an international driver's license.

Collect together all the documents you will need to pass through U.S. Customs and Border Protection.

Obtain some money in U.S. currency to use upon arrival in the U.S.

Confirm your flight in advance.

Read the airline's rules regarding any items you are not allowed to take on the airplane.

Pack your bags. It's time to go to America!!

Footnotes and Links: Chapter 4

(1) U.S. Immigration and Customs Enforcement (ICE). Student and Exchange Visitor Program (SEVP). https://studyinthestates.dhs.gov/us-immigration-and-customs-enforcement
(2) Study in the States. Who Is SEVP? https://studyinthestates.dhs.gov/2015/01/who-is-sevp
(3) Study in the States. Student Forms. https://studyinthestates.dhs.gov/student-forms?form=Forms_I-20
(4) Study in the States. Paying Your I-901 Service Fee. https://studyinthestates.dhs.gov/paying-your-i-901-sevis-fee
(5) U.S. State Department. Directory of Visa Categories. http://travel.state.gov/content/visas/en/general/all-visa-categories.html
(6) InternationalStudent.com Student Visas. http://www.internationalstudent.com/study_usa/preparation/student-visa/
(7) U.S. State Department. Visas. Visitor Visa Overview. http://travel.state.gov/content/visas/en/visit/visitor.html
(8) U.S. State Department. Consular Electronic Application Center. Apply for a Nonimmigrant Visa. https://ceac.state.gov/genniv/
(9) U.S. State Department. DS-160: Frequently Asked Questions. http://travel.state.gov/content/visas/en/forms/ds-160--online-nonimmigrant-visa-application/frequently-asked-questions.html
(10) U.S. State Department. Visas. Photo Requirements. http://travel.state.gov/content/visas/en/general/photos.html
(11) USEmbassy.gov. Websites of U.S. Embassies, Consulates and Diplomatic Missions. http://www.usembassy.gov/
(12) U.S. State Department. Visas. Visa Appointment & Processing Wait Times. http://travel.state.gov/content/visas/en/general/wait-times.html/
(13) U.S. State Department. Visas. Visitor Visa. Overview http://travel.state.gov/content/visas/en/visit/visitor.html

(14) U.S. State Department. Visas. Visa Denials. http://travel.state.gov/content/visas/en/general/denials.html#214b

(15) U.S. Consulate General of the United States. Shanghai, China. *Five Secrets of Applying for a U.S. Student Visa.* http://shanghai.usembassy-china.org.cn/students.html

(16) InternationalStudent.com Maintaining Your F1 Visa Status. http://www.internationalstudent.com/immigration/f1-student-visa/maintaining-your-f1-visa/

(17) U.S. State Department. Visas. Student Visas. https://travel.state.gov/content/visas/en/study-exchange/student.html

Chapter 5 – Welcome to the U.S.A.!

Your passport and visa are in hand, you have your immigration documents provided by the U.S. Consulate, and your I-20 form is ready to show to officials. You are carrying your I-901 receipt to prove that you've paid for a listing in the SEVIS database. Now you are ready to pack your luggage and say goodbye to your mom and dad, your best friend, and your dog (or cat).

Do some double-checking. Remember that your passport must be valid for at least six months after your arrival. Your visa must be correct and valid. The U.S. Consular Officer has given you a sealed envelope with your immigration papers. Do not open the sealed envelope. It will be opened upon your arrival by a Customs and Border Protection agent.

You are ready to travel! Getting to the U.S. is easy. Airplanes, trains, boats, buses, and cars all will bring you to America.

Arrival Procedures

Customs Declaration Form CF-6059

If you travel by air, you will be given a Customs Declaration form on the airplane (form CF-6059). This form is to declare certain items you may be carrying such as large amounts of currency, commercial merchandise, or other select items. A sample CF-6059 form can be found on the U.S. Customs and Border Protection website, Sample Customs Declaration Form page. (1) There are instructions on this sample form. If you do not understand how to complete the form, just ask the flight attendant for assistance. If you arrive by land or sea, you will be given a Customs Declaration form (CF-6059) by the Customs official when you arrival.

Upon arrival in the U.S., you will go through Customs and Border Protection which is part of the Department of Homeland Security. As you pass through Customs and Border Protection stations, carry with you these documents:

- your passport with visa;
- form I-20. Make three photocopies of this form;
- evidence of your financial resources such as a bank statement;
- letter of acceptance from your college;
- receipt for SEVIS payment (Form I-901);
- arrival/departure form I-94 (see below).

It is also recommended that you carry with you recent transcripts to prove your student status, the name of the college where you will study and the name of the DSO (designated school official) at your college with his/her contact information. Be sure to tell the agent that you have been accepted as a student and will be studying at this college.

Arrival and Departure Record Form I-94

Your next form is the I-94 form "Arrival and Departure Record." If you arrive by land, you will receive a paper copy of form I-94 upon arrival. If you come to America by sea or by air,

U.S. Customs and Border Protection (CBP) will generate an automated I-94 form. This record will be accessible online if you must prove your legal status to any authorities. (2) Be sure to a) determine that the information on this form is correct; and b) make note of your personal I-94 admission number and record it for safekeeping. When you leave the U.S., such as to travel to your home country, your departure will be recorded online using this I-94 number. U.S. Customs and Border Protection provides a factsheet about the I-94 automation process. (3)

Secondary Inspection Form I-515A

If your information cannot be verified by a Customs and Border Protection official upon arrival, you may be sent to a Secondary Inspection area. You will be interviewed in this separate location so as to not delay the arrival of other passengers. If you do not have all the necessary paperwork, you will be issued a form I-515A. This gives you temporary admittance to the U.S. You must provide the missing documentation within 30 days. If you do not, your visa will be cancelled and you will have to leave the U.S. immediately. Therefore, providing all required documentation within 30 days is a very serious matter. (4)

Summaries of Arrival Procedures

The U.S. Customs and Border Protection website provides general information for international visitors entering the United States (5). A more detailed description of the arrival procedures and required documentation is the U. S. Immigration and Customs Enforcement Fact Sheet, "What a Student or Exchange Visitor Can Expect Upon Arrival at a U.S. Port of Entry." (6)

We've discussed the forms you'll need when you arrive in the U.S. There may be some additional forms or documentation required by your college. An example is that the college may require you to show proof that you have been vaccinated against common illnesses such as measles. Ask the DSO (designated school official) about required forms and documents.

Travel Within the U.S.A.

Key Fact: You must report to your college within 30 days of arrival in the United States. This is very important. So plan your travel to arrive on time.

The U.S. Customs and Border Protection website lists all the ports of entry in the U.S. searchable by state. (7) This webpage shows not only the major ports of entry like San Francisco or New York City, and also those designated ports of entry in every state.

Unless your community college is quite near your port of entry airport, seaport or land border crossing, you are most likely going to be traveling within the U.S. to arrive at your community. You are probably going to be very tired from a long trip when you arrive. Maybe you flew from Shanghai to Los Angeles and the flight was 12 or 13 hours long! A very good idea is to arrange for an overnight stay near the airport so you can get some rest before you start traveling again.

Your F-1 student visa entitles you to travel within the United States. You also have a 60-day grace period after you finish your studies so that you may travel within the United States. If you decide to leave the U.S. temporarily while on an F1 student visa, you must obtain a B-2 visitor's visa or, if you are from country participating in the Visa Waiver Program, you must be registered with, and get approval from the **Electronic System for Travel Authorization (ESTA).** (8)

Of course, the location of your college will be the most important factor in how you travel within the U.S.

An Example: San Francisco, California, to Rock Springs, Wyoming

Let's use Rock Springs, Wyoming, for an example of domestic travel. Rock Springs is the home of Western Wyoming Community College. Let's imagine that you arrived from East Asia and your port of entry is San Francisco, California. Google is very good about finding ways to travel within the U.S. Be sure to search in the

English language. Go to www.Google.com and type "travel between San Francisco and Rock Springs, Wyoming" in the search box.

We learn that driving there in a car from San Francisco takes a little more than 13 hours. The distance is 919.8 miles. If you are not accustomed to using miles, you can convert miles to kilometers on the ConvertUnits.com website. (9) We quickly discover that the distance from San Francisco to Rock Springs is 1,480.2 kilometers.

Return to the Google page with the search links on ways to go to Rock Springs. Look at the many websites.

Domestic Flights

The Google search page provides many links to options for a flight between San Francisco and Rock Springs.

Here is a short list of websites that track different air companies and give you the best prices on flights between Rock Springs and San Francisco. You can also search the website of the airline company that flies to your destination.

Priceline.com http://www.priceline.com/insideTrack/flights/Rock_Springs-RKS-San_Francisco-SFO.html

Orbitz.com http://www.orbitz.com/flights/from-Rock_Springs-to-San_Francisco.o25824.d4468/

Flights.com http://www.flights.com/flights/rock-springs-rks-to-san-francisco-sfo/

FareCompare.com http://www.farecompare.com/flights/San_Francisco-SFO/Wyoming-WY/citystate.html#quote

Greyhound Bus

One of the links that appears for travel to Wyoming is the Greyhound bus website. (10) Greyhound is a national passenger bus line. We discover that it will cost you between $142 and $179 to travel between San Francisco and Rock Springs on a Greyhound bus. The price difference is related to when you travel. There's free Wi-Fi on Greyhound buses.

Train

Train travel is a very comfortable way to reach your destination in the U.S. Amtrak is the national passenger train service. (11) Unfortunately, trains are not as popular in many regions of the U.S. compared to other countries. Consequently, there are some destinations that have no train service. Rock Springs is a city with no Amtrak service.

However there are many other places that Amtrak trains will take you from San Francisco. On the Amtrak home page, click on Destinations. Choose the first option, which is California Train Routes. This takes you to a web page with a map and listing of train routes in and out of California. (12)

Perhaps your port of entry is Los Angeles, California. Click on that same California Train Routes page. See the table of different train lines. Click on the Texas Eagle line. (13) This Amtrak train line will take you to several cities with community colleges: Tucson, Arizona - Pima Community College; El Paso, Texas – El Paso Community College; San Antonio, Texas – San Antonio College; Dallas, Texas – several community colleges; Chicago, Illinois – more community colleges!

Traveling by train from Los Angeles to Chicago will be a long trip. But you will have the advantage of seeing a lot of the American West!

Keep in mind that the further east and northeast you go, the more train routes there are. So if your port of entry is New York City, you will have many options. This map (14) shows you train and bus stations that connect.

Other Options

Shuttles exist between many cities in the U.S. A shuttle is usually a ride in a 12-passenger van on the highway. There are several websites where you can book a shuttle between your airport and your destination. Examples are Shuttlefare.com, AirportShuttles.com, and GoAirportShuttle.com

Some colleges provide a shuttle service from the airport to the college. Here is just one example. Edmonds Community College in Lynnwood, Washington (north Seattle metro area), has an airport pickup and shuttle service. (15)

Finally, don't be shy about asking the DSO at your community college for advice. The community college may have some good ideas for you on the best way to reach your destination, and where to stay on your first night or nights in your new city, and how to seek more permanent housing.

In the next chapter 6, we'll look at academics and student life in the U.S.

Footnotes and Links: Chapter 5

(1) U.S. Customs and Border Protection. Sample Customs Declaration Form. http://www.cbp.gov/travel/us-citizens/sample-declaration-form

(2) U.S. Customs and Border Protection. Arrival/Departure Forms I-94 and I-94W. http://www.cbp.gov/travel/international-visitors/i-94-instructions

(3) U.S. Customs and Border Protection. I-94 Automation. https://studyinthestates.dhs.gov/sites/default/files/I-94_Fact_Sheet-3-22-13_v2.pdf

(4) Department of Homeland Security. Study in the States. *What is Form I-515A?* https://studyinthestates.dhs.gov/what-is-a-form-i-515a

(5) U.S. Customs and Border Protection. Travel. For International Visitors. http://www.cbp.gov/travel/international-visitors

(6) U. S. Immigration and Customs Enforcement Fact Sheet, "What a Student or Exchange Visitor Can Expect Upon Arrival at a U.S. Port of Entry." https://home.vef.gov/download/Fact_Sheet.pdf

(7) U.S. Customs and Border Protection. Locate a Port of Entry.
http://www.cbp.gov/contact/ports
(8) U.S. Department of Homeland Security. Study in the States.
Here to Help: U.S. Customs and Border Protection - Student
Travel While in the United States.
https://studyinthestates.dhs.gov/2012/12/here-to-help-us-customs-and-border-protection-student-travel-while-in-the-united-states
(9) ConvertUnits.com. Miles to Kilometers.
http://www.convertunits.com/from/miles/to/km
(10) Greyhound.com. Book a Trip.
https://www.greyhound.com/en/
(11) Amtrak.com. https://www.amtrak.com/home
(12) Amtrak.com. California Train Routes.
https://www.amtrak.com/california-train-routes
(13) Amtrak.com California Train Routes. Texas Eagle.
https://www.amtrak.com/texas-eagle-train
(14) Amtrak.com. Northeast Train-Bus Stations.
https://www.amtrak.com/northeast-train-bus-stations
(15) Edmonds Community College, Housing and Residence Life.
Arrival Information.
http://www.edcc.edu/housing/homestay-student/arrival-information.html

Chapter 6: Academics and Student Life

Steps to Enroll at Your Community College

You actually began the enrollment process long before arriving on campus. You did your research. You choose your community college, and you applied for admission. You were accepted. You applied for and obtained a visa, and you received and submitted several important forms required to enter the U.S. and to study at the college.

Next you provided your college with more required information such as the Affidavit of Support. You researched options for scholarships and financial aid, and applied for those relevant to your situation.

Finally you passed through U.S. Customs and Border Protection at your port of entry, and you've traveled to your campus. You are ready to become a student at an American community college!

Housing upon Arrival

Now is a good time to mention that you should arrange in advance housing for yourself that is available when you first arrive. You need a place to rest from your trip. You need a base from which to visit your campus. You need a place to stay while you begin looking for more permanent housing.

Some colleges have student dormitories. If you arranged with your college to stay in a dorm, then you can go directly to the dorm. Your college may have an arrangement for you to have temporary housing upon arrival. If not, you'll need to rent a motel or hotel room, or a home stay for a few nights. Ask your DSO what is available for temporary housing.

Some international students arrange long-term housing before they enter the U.S. For example, they may arrange for a home stay in the city where they will be living. Or they may decide to rent or lease an apartment in advance.

In the next chapter 7, Living in the U.S., we'll look more closely at renting/leasing an apartment or other types of housing during the time you are a student.

Check in and Show Your Immunization Documents

As soon as you have checked into your hotel, visit your DSO in the International Department at your community college. Let him or her know you have arrived. You will be given information to help you take the next steps.

At this visit to your DSO, you may also be asked to provide proof of immunization for several infectious diseases. At other colleges, the proof of immunization is required earlier, at the time you apply for admission. Typically, this immunization proof is required of all students, not just international students. For example, Colorado Mountain College is required by Colorado state law to get immunization proof for measles, mumps, and rubella vaccination from all student applicants. Colorado Mountain College includes this requirement on its admissions checklist. (1) Austin Community College in Austin, Texas, requires all students under the age of 22 to be immunized against meningitis. (2) This vaccination is required by Texas state law.

Each college has its own requirements so be sure to ask your DSO about documenting your vaccinations. The DSO will also have information on where to get immunization shots if you need one.

Your next step is to visit the Assessment Center.

Assessment Tests

Most community colleges require all students, including international students, to take **assessment tests** before enrolling in a class. These assessment tests evaluate basic reading, writing, and math skills, as well as English-proficiency levels. At some colleges, the tests are referred to as **placement tests** because students will be "placed" in a class appropriate to their current skill level. International students typically provide TOEFL scores or scores from another English-language test at the time of application to prove that they are proficient in English However, if the international student's TOEFL score is below a designated level, the student will also be given an assessment test in English proficiency so that the students will each be placed in the best class for their skill level.

Let's look at some examples.

Bunker Hill Community College has an Assessment Center with full information about testing using the College Placement Test (CPT) system. (3) There's even information on how to prepare for the CPT. (4) Bunker Hill also provides an English-proficiency test just for international students called the LOEP (Levels of English Proficiency). (5) Students are placed in ESL classes at different levels based on the results of this test.

Washtenaw Community College in Ann Arbor, Michigan, refers to its placement test series as the COMPASS Placement Test (Computer-Adaptive Placement Assessment and Support System). On its website, the college provides website information on how and where to take the test, how to prepare, and even how to deal with test anxiety. (6)

Santa Barbara City College has an Assessment Center that provides information on placement tests, both academic and ESL. The Assessment Center gives you some examples of test questions and sample practice tests. (7) Normandale Community College in the Minneapolis/St. Paul, Minnesota, metro area provides complete information about placement tests. This includes detailed information on how to understand your test scores. (8)

Pima Community College in Tucson, Arizona, also provides full information about assessment tests, including a FAQ sheet and sample questions. (9) Pima CC also provides "**brush-up**" workshops to help you practice and prepare for the tests. In addition, Pima Community College's Assessment Center provides Challenge Exams. If you do well on a Challenge Exam, you can move past a lower level course and enroll instead in a higher-level course. Biology and chemistry are given as examples. The college explains that passing a Challenge Exam will "accelerate your progress toward your degree or certificate." (10)

Keep in mind that if you do not provide TOEFL scores, and if you do not do well on English proficiency assessment tests, you will be required to enroll in ESL courses first. Later, as your English improves, you will be allowed to enroll in the academic courses that will count toward your degree such as math, science, English composition, etc. Check your community college website for information about these options, or ask your DSO.

CLEP Exams and AP Exams

While you are taking those assessment test, you might want to consider taking a CLEP exam or an AP exam, both of which can earn you college credits in your academic program.

CLEP Exams

College Level Examination Program (CLEP) is a credit-by-examination program that provides tests over several subject areas. If you pass the CLEP test, you may full credit for the course that the test covers. You can save yourself both time and money if you are successful with your CLEP exam because you will get credit for a course that you do not have to take. You can save hundreds of dollars in tuition on that particular course. You will earn course credit for required courses, and the course credits may transfer when you move to your four-year university after finishing your associate degree.

CLEP exams are a project of the College Board, the same organization that provides SAT and ACT college entrance examinations. According to the College Board website, nearly 3,000 American colleges and universities accept credits achieved by passing a CLEP exam. (11) Some 33 exams are available in five categories: history and social sciences, composition and literature, science and mathematics, business, and world languages. Examples in the business category include financial accounting, information systems, introductory business law, principles of management, and principles of marketing. French, German, and Spanish are the only world languages currently being tested.

CLEP exams cost only a fraction of the tuition for the same course. CLEP exams usually cost $80; for an additional $10, students can purchase a preparatory guide. As you can see, $80 for the test is far less expensive than paying for tuition for the same course, and you'll save time, too. However CLEP exams are not easy. Prepare well!

It's a good idea to investigate which CLEP exam scores will be accepted by the four-year college or university that you plan to attend after community college. For example, California community colleges have transfer agreements with the California State University branches (there are several branches including Fresno, Long Beach, Sacramento, etc.). California State University lists the courses on its website with CLEP exam equivalents. (12) Or you can check first with the DSO at your community college. Your community college website will have information, too, about CLEP exams. Here is an example: Valencia College in Orlando, Florida (13).

An easy strategy is to look at the College Board website on CLEP exams. The Getting Started page has a search function to find your college and learn its policy regarding CLEP exams, which exams are offered, when, and where. (14)

Key point: CLEP scores do not necessarily transfer automatically to your four-year university. You may have to arrange yourself for the CLEP scores to be sent at the same time that you send your community college transcripts.

AP Exams

The College Board also provides **Advanced Placement (AP)** exams for students. Typically, these are tests taken by high school students in the U.S. who have taken courses in a specific subject area. Students not in the U.S. can take AP exams, too. Like CLEP exams, passing an AP exam means you may get college course credit for that course.

Very often, you'll find information about CLEP exams and AP exams in the same place. For example, Bunker Hill Community College has information about both these exams. (15) Learn more about AP exams from the College Board's website. (16) Advanced Placement tests are available only in May, whereas CLEP exams are available year round.

Check with your DSO to learn which test or tests your college offers.

Academic Advising

What You Need to Know

To earn a degree from an American college, you must complete certain **required courses**. Other courses that are not required are called **elective courses**. Your first step is to determine which courses are required to earn a degree. You will want to read a description of the required and elective courses. Then you must learn if any of those required course will be offered in the upcoming semester or quarter.

Colleges usually provide a college catalog that covers all aspects of college life, policies and rules, admission information, faculty listings, and also the requirements for earning a degree. The college catalog is often offered both as a printed catalog, and a digital version is also posted on the college website. The catalog typically lists the specific courses you must complete in order to earn a degree in your chosen field. New versions of the catalog are published frequently, often every year.

For example, Kingsborough Community College in New York City provides on its website the most current catalog and past versions as well. (17) Looking at Kingsborough's 2015-2016 catalog, we can find the degree program that we want to study. Let's use an associate degree in biotechnology, or an associate in business administration as examples. In the Kingsborough college catalog you will find exactly which courses are required to complete in order to earn those two degrees. You'll also find elective courses as well.

Santa Monica College in Santa Monica, California, provides another detailed example. Santa Monica has its college catalog for 2015-2016 posted on its website. (18) You can download the entire catalog or just parts of it, depending upon what you want to know. Let's look at one part of the catalog available to download from this page, Course Descriptions. Each course listed in this document has a name, a number, and a description. Course descriptions include the number of credits you will earn, what topics the course covers, and if the course transfers to a specific transfer partner. The course description also tells you if there is a prerequisite. A **prerequisite** is a course you must complete before you take the course being described. For example, if you want to take Accounting Ethics, the prerequisite is to have taken either Accounting 1 (Introduction to Financial Accounting) or Accounting 21 (Business Bookkeeping). Accounting 1 and 21 do not have prerequisites because they are basic courses.

Which of these many courses in the catalog are required for your chosen degree? Santa Monica College has provided a document on this same college catalog page titled Majors and Areas of Interest. This document provides very detailed information about which courses you must take to graduate and which are required for transfer to one of Santa Monica College's California university transfer partners.

Now you need to know if a specific course will be available or when it will become available. That's because many courses are taught only once a year, not every semester. You must look at the

Class Schedule page on the Santa Monica College website. (19) This is a searchable page. You enter your course title and you will be given information about where and when the class will be taught and by whom. Note the column that has a "Closed" or "Open" designation. **Closed** means that only a pre-determined number of students is allowed in this class, and the class is already full. **Open** means that there are still places available, and you can register for the class.

International students at Cabrillo College, California

Every community college has this kind of information available: the courses required for a specific degree, description of courses, and availability of courses. But each college handles this information differently. Look carefully at your college's website.

Academic Advising Process

The role of academic advising is to learn from an experienced academic advisor or counselor at your college all of the information we just covered in the previous paragraphs. You will meet face-to-face with an academic advisor or communicate personally online to discuss your academic goals. You will discuss degree requirements for your **major**, which courses you must take to earn the degree, and when those courses will be offered. The advisor gives you additional information on adding a course or dropping a course, or withdrawing from a course.

A meeting with your academic advisor is a great place to ask questions. If you've been confused by something you saw in the college catalog, now is the time to ask. It is the job of the academic advisor to help you have a successful experience as a student.

To get an idea of how academic advising works, take a look at the community college websites: Northern Virginia Community College (20); Harper College (21); Colorado Mountain College (22); and Pima Community College. (23)

Orientation and Registration

Many community colleges require new students to attend an orientation session. The idea behind **orientation** is to orient you – to point you in the right direction so you will be heading toward your goals. The orientation may be an actual gathering of students led by advisors or the orientation may be online – or a combination of both.

Also you will be required to sign up for the college's online web services for students. There you will be able to receive email and participate in online discussions with your professor and fellow students. You can also manage your college account and pay tuition using this online college service.

At the orientation, you will be shown how to register for classes. Many colleges now provide online registration. This means you should have reviewed which courses you must take for your degree, and you should have spoken with an advisor. At the same time, many colleges also continue to provide a "walk-in" registration for students who prefer to register in person.

Keep in mind that class rosters change frequently at the beginning of each semester. If you find that a class you wanted is "closed," then watch the online registration. If a student drops out, then the class will become "open" again. You can "**add**" this course to your current semester's registration if it has become open again. Frequently there is a **"wait list"** for a class that is in demand. You have to wait until you name comes up to the top of the wait list.

You will pay your fees when your registration process is completed. **Fees** include tuition and also additional fees for science laboratory classes, library services, activity center usage, technology usage, etc. Fees vary from college to college. As mentioned, you may be able to pay online through the college's online student web service. Most colleges also accept personal checks on your bank account or charges to your credit card. We'll discuss how to handle money (banks, credit cards, saving money) in the next chapter 7, Living in the U.S.

Now You Are a Student!

You've been advised, you've attended orientation, you've registered for your classes, you have your class schedule in hand, and you've paid your tuition and fees. You are now a college student!!

Maintain Your Visa Status

Keep in mind that you must maintain your visa status while you are studying at an American community college.

Students who fail to enroll in courses at the community college where they were accepted, or who do not enroll as full-time students (at least 12 credit hours) are in violation of their visa status. You must also maintain a GPA (grade point average) of at least 2.0 and complete at least 67% of your courses. Your I-20 form must be current.

The U.S. Department of Homeland Security maintains a website, Study in the States, that has a page with full information about maintaining your visa status. (24) Another excellent source of information is the InternationalStudent.com website's page Maintaining Your F1 Visa Status. (25)

Coming Up

In the next chapters, you'll look at several topics relevant to living in the U.S. such as housing, transportation, and shopping. You'll also learn more about American culture and traditions, and how to deal with cultural shock and homesickness.

Footnotes and Links: Chapter 6

(1) Colorado Mountain College. Admissions Checklist.
http://coloradomtn.edu/admissions/applying/admissions_checklist/
(2) Austin Community College. Meningitis Compliance Steps.
http://www.austincc.edu/apply-and-register/enrollment-steps/comply-with-meningitis-law/meningitis-compliance-steps
(3) Bunker Hill Community College. Assessment Center.
http://www.bhcc.mass.edu/assessment/
(4) Bunker Hill Community College. Preparing for the CPT.
http://www.bhcc.mass.edu/cptpractice/
(5) Bunker Hill Community College. English as a Second Language (ESL).
http://www.bhcc.mass.edu/assessment/englishasasecondlanguage/
(6) Washtenaw Community College. Placement Testing.
http://www.wccnet.edu/studentconnection/placement/
(7) Santa Barbara City College. Placement Center. Sample Test Questions.
http://www.sbcc.edu/assessmentcenter/sampletestquestions.php
(8) Normandale Community College. Placement Testings.
http://www.normandale.edu/admissions/placement-testing

(9) Pima Community College. Take Assessments.
https://www.pima.edu/new-students/take-assessments/index.html
(10) Pima Community College. Challenge Exams.
https://www.pima.edu/new-students/take-assessments/challenge-exams.html
(11) College Board. CLEP. https://clep.collegeboard.org/
(12) The California State University. CSU Student Transfer. The College Level Examination Program (CLEP).
http://calstate.edu/transfer/requirements/TheCollegeLevelExaminationProgramCLEP.shtml
(13) Valencia College. Assessment Services. College Level Examination Program (CLEP).
http://valenciacollege.edu/assessments/clep/
(14) College Board. Get Started with CLEP.
https://clep.collegeboard.org/started
(15) Bunker Hill Community College. Prior Learning Assessment.
http://www.bhcc.mass.edu/priorlearningassessment/
(16) College Board. AP Students.
https://apstudent.collegeboard.org/home?navid=ap-aps
(17) Kingsborough Community College. College Catalog.
http://www.kbcc.cuny.edu/sub-registration/Pages/catalog.aspx
(18) Santa Monica College. Santa Monica College Catalog 2015-2016. http://www.smc.edu/CollegeCatalog/Pages/default.aspx
(19) Santa Monica College. Class Schedules.
http://www.smc.edu/AboutSMC/Pages/Class-Schedules.aspx
(20) Northern Virginia Community College. Advising and Counseling. https://www.nvcc.edu/advising/
(21) Harper College, Academic Advising and Counseling.
http://goforward.harpercollege.edu/services/advising/
(22) Colorado Mountain College. Academic Advising.
http://coloradomtn.edu/student_services/advising/
(23) Pima Community College. Academic Advising.
https://www.pima.edu/current-students/advising/

(24) U.S. Department of Homeland Security. Study in the States. Maintaining Your Status.
https://studyinthestates.dhs.gov/maintaining-your-status
(25) InternationalStudents.com. Maintaining Your F1 Visa.
http://www.internationalstudent.com/immigration/f1-student-visa/maintaining-your-f1-visa/

Chapter 7 Living in the U.S.

International students must make the same living arrangements that anyone in the United States must make. Handling money and paying your bills, arranging for housing, arranging for transportation, getting health care, and going shopping will be a big part of your life in the United States. In this chapter, we'll look at each of these daily living topics. We'll also consider ways to save money.

Money

Currency

U.S. currency is based on the tens system. Each dollar has 100 cents. The smallest coin is the penny and it is worth one cent. Next is the nickel which is worth five cents. The dime is worth ten cents and the quarter is worth 25 cents. Occasionally we see a one-dollar coin but paper currency for $1 is much more common. Typically we see one- five-, ten-, and twenty-dollar paper **bills** of currency. Larger denominations are available at banks. We refer to coins and paper currency as **cash**.

Bank Accounts/Credit Unions/ATMs/Debit Cards

International students often open a bank account at an American bank prior to arriving in the U.S. or immediately upon arrival. Most banks allow you to wire money from your bank in your home country to deposit in your new bank account in the U.S. There is usually a fee to wire money. Find a bank in the U.S. that is easy for you to access and that has a website with full services.

Banks typically offer two basic types of accounts, **checking** and **savings**. Checking accounts may or may not pay you interest on your **bank balance** (the amount in your account). You can pay your **bills** by writing a check. The recipient of the check will deposit your check into the recipient's bank account. Your bank will transfer funds to the recipient's account, and the amount will be withdrawn from your checking account. If someone pays you with a check, you must **endorse** the check by signing your name on the back of the check. Then you deposit the check in your account. Savings accounts will pay you a small amount each month in interest on the total amount in your savings account. Banks often limit the number of withdrawals you can make from a savings account each month.

Another way to pay bills is to set up an online account and give the recipient access to your bank account. Examples are paying your **utility bills**, paying credit card bills, etc. Be careful! Be sure that the website for the online account is secure. You don't want your bank account information and your money to be stolen.

You can also pay bills by going to the office of the company or organization that has billed you, or by mailing a check as payment. Large grocery stores offer payment services for utilities and other bills.

An alternative to a bank is a **credit union**. A credit union is a financial institution owned by its members. Credit unions function in many of the same ways as banks. For example, credit unions have checking and savings accounts and can make loans to members. Membership is usually restricted to members of a specific community, such as all the employees of a corporation or a school district. Or membership can be available for residents of a particular county or city. Many universities have credit unions for employees and students.

Most American banks and credit unions provide customers a **credit card** to use to buy items directly from a merchant or to use with an **ATM (automatic teller machine)**. You can go to the ATM, insert your card into the ATM, then type in your **PIN number** on a keypad. The ATM will release cash, and the amount will be withdrawn from your account.

Also you can buy items in stores using a **debit card**. For example, you go to the grocery store to buy food. When you check out, instead of paying cash or using a credit card, you insert your debit card, enter your PIN number, and the amount is automatically removed from your checking account. Debit cards are not **credit cards**. Don't forget to write in your check book where you used the debit card and how much money was removed.

Traveler's checks are another way of handling money. You purchase traveler's checks at your bank. Then when you arrive at your destination in another country, you will go to a bank that accepts traveler's checks. You can convert the traveler's check into local currency. Traveler's checks are being gradually replaced by ATM, credit cards, and debit cards.

InternationalStudent.com has some tips about how to choose a bank and which kinds of accounts to choose. (1) Note that this website advises you to bring about $2,000 in cash when you arrive in the U.S. to use until you can transfer more money to your new U.S. bank account. This can be brought as traveler's checks or as a bank card from your home country bank. Determine first if your bank card will work at an American ATM machine.

Never leave large amounts of cash money in your dormitory room or your apartment. Put that money in the bank where it will be much safer. Cash that is stolen is lost forever.

Changing money from your home currency to U.S. currency is often most easily done at the airport when you arrive. If you convert foreign currency at your local bank in your destination city, the conversion rate may not be as good, if it's even possible.

Paying Bills: Credit Cards, PayPal etc.

As we've just discussed, you can pay your bills by writing a check on your bank checking account. Then you mail the check or take it to a payment location.

Credit cards are a very common way of paying for bills in the U.S. You can pay at the store with a credit card when you make a purchase. It's easy to get a credit card for Americans, and less easy for international students with no credit history. You will probably be asked repeatedly by many companies to get your credit card from them. The most common companies are Visa, MasterCard, Discover, and American Express. You simply fill out forms and establish an account.

When you want to purchase something online, you simply choose your credit card account to pay. When your credit card statement arrives in the mail, the statement will show all your purchases for the billing period.

Keep in mind that credit card companies charge very high interest rates on accounts that are not paid in full every month. Try to pay the entire amount you owe each month so you can avoid high interest fees

Another way to make a purchase online is to use PayPal or another online payment system. **PayPal** is similar to AliPay in China. You establish an account online at the PayPal.com website. When you want to purchase something, instead of clicking on credit card payment, you choose PayPal to pay. Then PayPal will charge your credit card account. The value of PayPal and similar systems is that you only have one account – PayPal – for many vendors. You can avoid giving your personal credit card number to every vendor.

There are several alternatives to PayPal. For example, Google Wallet is a payment system that is growing in popularity. Search Engine Journal has information about 12 alternatives to PayPal. (2)

It is important to be sure that your online payments system, either credit card or other system, is secure. You do not want you financial information stolen! When you go to "check out" and pay for your purchase online, look at the URL of the online payments system. Does it have a green color lock shape? That green lock means the payment system is secure.

Wikipedia has a good article on these different "e-commerce" payment systems so that you have a more comprehensive understanding. (3)

Time and Dates

Unlike people in many countries, Americans record dates by month, day, and year rather than starting with the year. An example is, "I wrote this letter on May 4, 2016."

The United States is divided into east-west **time zones.** We start in the Eastern Time Zone in the eastern U.S. and move west through the Central Time Zone, then farther west to the Mountain Time Zone, and then to the Pacific Time Zone on the West Coast. As we move west, the time on the clock moves back one additional hour. So when it is nine in the morning in Boston, the time in the Central zone is 8 in the morning, 7 in the morning in the Mountain zone, and 6 in the morning in the Pacific zone. These four zones refer to only the mainland United States. There are actually nine time zones that include places such as Alaska, Hawaii, and Puerto Rico.

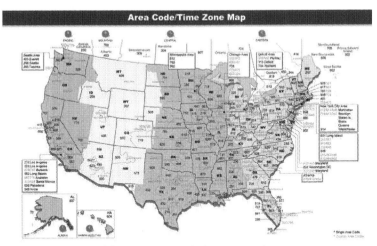

Time zones and telephone area codes

Even more confusing, many states follow **Daylight Saving Time**. The clock is moved back one hour in autumn, and returns forward one hour in spring. Or you might say the standard time is the autumn and winter time and the hour "springs forward" one hour in spring and summer. These time zones coordinate with the Greenwich Mean Time Zone in England. The Eastern Time Zone is five hours earlier than Greenwich Mean Time in England. So when it's midnight/12 a.m. in Boston, it is already 7 a.m. in England.

Americans note the time differently than in other countries. Instead of counting a 24-hour day, Americans start over after 12 hours. Instead of noting the Mountain Time Zone of 19:08 in Denver, Colorado, Americans will tell you that it's 7:08 p.m. The notation a.m. is before noon; p.m. starts at noon and goes to midnight, then we go back to a.m. A.M. means ante meridiem (before midday) and p.m. means post meridiem (after midday).

Why is all this time craziness important to you? If you are scheduled to talk to an admissions officer at a university in another time zone, you need to know what time it is where you are calling. Or if you are applying for a job, you want to know the time where the job interviewer is. Note, too, that several U.S. states are divided into two time zones. If you are calling home to China or Germany or Ethiopia, you also want to know what time it is where you are calling.

For the record, many Americans are not happy with all this, especially the Daylight Saving Time changes. Furthermore, not all states follow Daylight Saving Time! Maybe this will change but for now we're stuck with this.

Wikipedia has good articles that explain the time zones (4) and Daylight Savings Time. (5) Of course, the easiest way to find out what time it is elsewhere is to go to the World Clock-Worldwide. Find your city or a city in your time zone listed on the clock, and then find the city that you want to call. (6)

How we handle time is an important factor in any culture. Americans usually expect you to appear at business and social events on time. College classes start on time as well. Job interviews start on time, too. So be sure to appear a few minutes before your appointed time. You must also pay your rent and your utility bills (electricity, water, gas) on time, usually on the first of the month.

On the other hand, some appointments are often late. Doctors and dentists usually make you wait 15 to 30 minutes before you see the doctor. Many government agencies also often require you to wait because the officials in the agency have fallen behind schedule.

Housing

On-campus housing in a dormitory is common on university campuses, but not so common on two-year community college campuses. If living on-campus in a dormitory appeals to you, ask you college DSO if there are dormitory options.

Host family housing is another option. If you choose this option, you will stay with an American family. Meals may or may not be provided. You will pay a pre-set amount each month for this living arrangement. Note that some colleges refer to "host families" to indicate social opportunities with an American family – not living arrangements.

It is far more common for international students to live off-campus in an apartment, duplex, or rental house. Apartment living is the most common. A duplex is a building that has two apartments, one on each side of the building. A rental house is simply as described. It is a house for rent, often with two or more bedrooms. You will want to find roommates to share space and rental fees if you choose a larger rental unit.

Apartments can be located in large multi-apartment buildings, or attached to a smaller building like a house. Some apartments are **furnished** (already have furniture) and others are **unfurnished**. You find apartments for rent by looking in classified ads in the newspaper, in online listings like **Craig's List**, or announcements in school newspapers and bulletin boards. Call the **landlord** and arrange to meet. Sometimes the landlord is referred to as the **manager**. If you like the apartment, you will pay a **deposit** to the landlord or manager. This deposit assures the landlord that any damage to the apartment while you are living there will be paid for in advance. For example, if you punch a hole in wall (!), the deposit will pay for fixing this damage. The deposit also often includes the last month's rent. You also have to pay the first month's rent. Consequently, your first payment to the landlord can be rather large because it includes the damage deposit plus first and last month's rental fee.

You will most likely be required to sign a **lease.** A lease is a legal document that outlines your obligation to the landlord and the landlord's obligation to you. For example, tenants are required to keep the property free of damage, to not have wild, loud parties, to pay rent on time each month, etc. The landlord is required in the lease to fix faulty or broken furnaces, air conditioners, and major appliances like refrigerators, and to fix stopped-up plumbing, etc.

Some apartments include all or some **utilities** in the monthly rental free. Utilities include gas, electricity, garbage pick-up, and cable television. Many apartments have free Wi-Fi for internet access.

If you have children or pets, check with the landlord first to see if they are allowed. Some apartments allow pets but require a higher deposit to cover pet-caused damage.

All these topics are questions to ask the landlord/manager. You will want to know exactly what services your rent covers, and what it does not cover. Read the lease carefully.

When choosing an apartment, also consider where the apartment is in relation to your campus, to shopping, and to transportation. If you ride a city bus to campus every day, where is the bus route in relationship to your apartment? How far from the nearest grocery store is your apartment? Is there free Wi-Fi? Don't be shy about asking!!

Telephone, Television, and Internet Access

Telephone service is available by way of land lines in American cities and towns. However landlines with wall phone jacks are not available in as many places as we've seen in the past. Cell phone service is growing more popular yearly as well.

More than 90 percent of Americans pay for their television service. They subscribe to television channels on cable, dish satellite or through their phone company. Subscriber services such as Netflix bring films and television programs to your home. In larger cities with television stations that broadcast signals, it is possible to purchase an antenna and watch television for free. However, the number of stations received is limited when using an antenna compared to cable and satellite TV. Only 7 per cent of Americans use this "over the air" method of receiving television signals.

Internet access is typically through a telephone or cable TV service. Fees are charged for this service. However, some apartments offer free Wi-Fi internet service as part of the rental agreement.

Ask your DSO or fellow students about the best methods of receiving television and internet access in your home, and the best companies for cell phone service.

Transportation

Like all students, your options for transportation in the U.S. include taking city buses or in larger cities, subways and light-rail trains; bicycling, walking, or driving a car. How you get to school every day will depend on what form of transportation you have available. This will have a direct impact on your choice of college. If you choose a college in a cold climate with heavy winter snows, bicycling is probably not going to be your best way to get to school. Walking will be difficult, too, unless the school is really close to your apartment.

When you choose a community college, also take time to learn something about the transportation options in that city. Typically, cities have information online about their bus systems. Let's look at a couple of examples by doing a Google search for the name of your chosen city and the phrase "metro bus service." You will quickly find that most mid-size and larger cities in the U.S. have extensive bus services, and larger cities also have subway and light-rail service.

Driving a Car

Driving in the U.S. means you have to buy or lease a car. Purchasing and operating a car is expensive. You are required by law to have a driver's license and insurance on your vehicle. So be prepared to pay for the convenience of driving.

If you already have an international driver's license, you may use it while in the U.S. You will not be required to get an additional license. Therefore, you should consider getting an international driver's license before entering the U.S.

If you do not have a driver's license, you will be required to get one in the U.S. state where you are living. Your first step is to acquire a Social Security number (see below under Working in the U.S. for more information about Social Security). Each state has a Department of Transportation with a Motor Vehicle Division (DMV), that is responsible for its citizens' driver's licenses. To get a driver's license, you must pass both a written test and a driving test. You will be given a printed manual with the laws and guidelines for driving to study before you take the written test. In the driving test, you will drive your car accompanied by a Department of Transportation employee who will give you directions and judge your driving performance.

When you go to the Division of Motor Vehicles (DMV) for testing, you will be required to bring certain documents such as your passport and visa. Some states require a Social Security number. The specific documents that you must take with you vary from state to state, so ask in advance which documents you should bring. Once you pass the tests and a vision test as well as pay the required fee, you will receive your **driver's license**. The Department of Homeland Security's Study in the United States website provides a guide to getting a driver's license. (7)

Purchasing a car is a big financial investment. Read about how to choose a car in advance. *Consumer Reports* magazine has good articles about the different brands of cars, their safety record, repair and maintenance costs, etc.

When you purchase a car, you will receive a paper called the **title** to the car. This paper proves that you are now owner of the car. Next you must **register** the car with the state where you live, typically at the local Division of Motor Vehicles office. There is a fee associated with registering the car. You will receive **license plates** to put on the car to identify the car.

You are also required to purchase **auto insurance**. The minimum insurance required by law is called **liability insurance**. If you are in involved in a traffic accident, and the accident is your fault, the liability insurance will pay for damage to the car that you hit and health-care costs for the person in that car. But liability insurance will not pay for damage to your car or for your health-care costs. To get coverage for yourself, you must purchase insurance with greater coverage.

We can conclude that buying, licensing, insuring, and maintaining a car is a very expensive business.

Keep in mind that you required to keep proof of registration and insurance in the car. If you are stopped by the police for a traffic violation, you will be asked to show the registration and proof of insurance.

Never forget that you are required to follow all laws regarding driving a motor vehicle. If you do not follow the laws and are caught by police, you may have to pay a large monetary fine, or worse.

Shopping

Shopping for food and household items like soap is usually done at a grocery store, and these items are referred to as **groceries**. Small **convenience stores** will have a few food items such as snacks or soft drinks. Large grocery stores are called

supermarkets, and these stores have a wide range of food and household items. Supermarkets have the regular offering of dairy products, meats, fruits and vegetables, and canned and boxed foods. Supermarkets also often include a bakery and alcoholic beverage shop. **Pharmacies** are also common in large supermarkets.

Many cities have a chain of grocery stores, all run by the same company. There are also large retail stores like Walmart and Costco that sell many different items, including groceries. The stores often have "specials," which are printed advertisements of weekly sales on common grocery items.

Larger cities or cities with big populations of ethnic minorities will have **ethnic markets**. For example, Tucson, Arizona, has several ethnic minorities. As a consequence, Tucson has ethnic grocery stores specializing in Asian, Mexican, and Middle Eastern foods.

Health food stores offer **produce** (fresh fruit and vegetables) that is organically-grown. They may sell eggs, milk products, and/or meats that are produced without antibiotics or growth hormones. Vitamins, minerals, and other nutritional supplements are often sold at these stores as well.

Other items you may need for yourself or your apartment can be purchased at a variety of stores – from large shopping malls with many stores, **"big box" stores** such as WalMart, K-Mart, and Target, to small neighborhood stores. Specialty stores such as **hardware stores** offers a variety of tools, garden supplies, paint, and lighting options.

If you are on a tight budget, you can save money in several ways. **Thrift stores** are usually operated by charitable organizations. The items in the store are used and donated. Household items, clothing, tools, and furniture are cleaned and repaired and offered for sale. Americans like to have **garage sales**, also called **yard sales**, at their homes on the weekends. They sell old items like furniture, books, and clothing – often for very low prices.

Craig'sList is another option for finding good deals on a wide variety of items from used cars to baby beds to a new apartment. Craig'sList also has personal notices, job notices, housing options, discussion forums, and services and goods for sale. There is a Craig'sList in many cities around the world, but most are in the U.S. This website has a Craig'sList locator so that you can find the Craig'sList in your town. (8). Or you can simply put into the Google search box the phrase Craig'sList and name of your town. Example: Craig'sList Las Cruces, New Mexico. The Craig'sList site for Las Cruces will quickly appear. Warning! Craig'sList has no moderator to check the listings for honesty. There are scams on Craig'sLists. A **scam** is an effort to cheat or defraud someone. Read the Craig's List warning on how to avoid scams before you attempt to purchase anything. (9)

You can also save money when shopping for textbooks. There are several websites that sell new and used texts at lower prices, and also digital copies of textbooks. Another option is to rent a textbook for the semester you are enrolled in the class. Consumer Reports has a good guide to saving money on textbooks. (10)

Health Care and Emergencies

Purchasing health insurance is very important for any individual living in the United States. The cost of health care is extremely high and can ruin you financially if you do not have health insurance to pay for some of the costs. Health insurance is complicated. Usually your health insurance will pay for most of your health care expenses, but you will have to pay part of the total costs. Many community colleges provide health insurance for students and require that you sign up for it.

A really excellent video, *U.S. Healthcare System Overview*, that explains the health care system and health care insurance can be found on the Austin Community College website. (11) It has a lot of details so you may want to watch it twice. This video reminds you to bring with you from your home country any prescriptions you have and a supply of medications you need. If possible, get dental care, vision care, and a general health examination before entering the U.S.

Prescriptions can be filled at pharmacies in the U.S. that are located as separate businesses or in larger grocery stores.

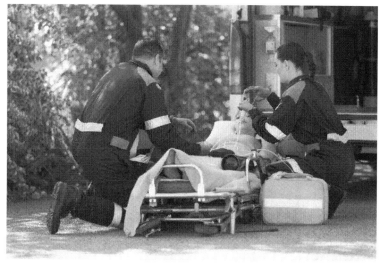

Emergency services

If you find that you have an emergency medical problem such as a sudden, severe illness or an accident with injuries, then call the telephone number 9-1-1. You will be required to describe the problem if you can, and where you are located. Emergency medical technicians and an ambulance will be sent to you. You will be transported to the emergency room of a nearby hospital for further medical care.

Better is to anticipate any health problem and seek care at your college's health care center or at an urgent care center (walk-in clinic). These provide health care at far less expense than going to the emergency room.

Working in the U.S.

On Campus Jobs

An international student with the F-1 visa may work at a job on the campus of his/her college after completion of a full semester of classes. Students are authorized to work a maximum of 20 hours in these on-campus jobs. The pay for these jobs is usually low, and income from these jobs should be viewed as supplementary. The jobs are varied and very likely will not be related to your chosen field of study. Students must receive written authorization from the college before beginning an on-campus job.

Off-Campus Jobs

There are four possibilities for off-campus jobs: 1) Optional Practical Training (OPT); 2) Curricular Practical Training (CPT); 3) an internship with an international organization; 4) economic hardship.

Optional Practical Training (OPT) is available to students who have completed their college course work or who have been pursuing a degree for more than nine months. Keep in mind that you must apply for OPT before you have finished your degree. You can work up to 40 hours a week in an OPT job. Students may extend their F-1 visas to work in OPT jobs related to their fields of study, and thus getting on-the-job training that will be beneficial when they seek permanent employment. For students in STEM (Science, Technology, Engineering and Mathematics) fields, a 17-month extension is allowed. For more information about OPT, see the U.S. Citizenship and Immigration Services website. (12) As mentioned in an earlier chapter, an example of OPT placement is at Pima Community College in Tucson, Arizona. The college has facilitated OPT placement in Tucson high-tech firms for students in business and graphics fields.

Curricular Practical Training (CPT) refers to jobs that are integrated into the curriculum of a specific college class. You will

103

get on-the-job training for your chosen field. Your college handles these training programs. Talk to your DSO for more information.

An internship with international organizations refers to temporary employment in your professional field. The job must be with an organization authorized to accept student interns. Examples are the United Nation or the World Bank. You can have an internship with an international organization, and later also apply for OPT.

Severe economic hardship is not simply about not having enough money. Individuals who qualify for this category once had the needed funds but lost them due to an unfortunate event. An example would be a sudden devaluation of your home country's currency that reduces your financial resources. Another example is sudden loss of your on-campus job through no fault of your own. This status of severe economic hardship is difficult and time-consuming to prove. U.S. Citizenship and Immigration Service must approve your hardship status. It can take up to three months for processing this application.

A good overview with details plus a video explanation of these employment options is available at InternationalStudent.com (13) and (14) More information is available from the Study in States, Department of Homeland Security. (15)

Working off-campus requires authorization from the U.S. Citizenship and Immigration Services, which is part of the U.S. Department of Homeland Security. You must apply for employment authorization by filing form I-765. This form with instructions can be found on the U.S. Citizenship and Immigration Services website. (16) Form I-765 applies to OPT jobs, internships, and cases of economic hardship.

Failure to get proper approval to work puts you in danger of losing your F-1 status, so be sure to follow the rules, fill out the forms, and meet the requirements!

Social Security

Keep in mind that before seeking employment, either on- or off-campus, you must have acquired Social Security card with your personal Social Security number. You must wait at least 10 days after arriving in the U.S. before you apply. You go to the nearest Social Security office to fill out the forms. Study in the States provides information about the steps you must follow (17), and as does the Social Security Administration. (18)

Next Up

In this chapter, we've learned how to manage money and pay bills, arrange for housing and transportation, get health care, and maybe even find a job. Once all these "living" tasks are taken care of, in the next chapter we'll consider some aspects of American culture, what you may want to do to fit in, and how American culture may affect you and your experience in the U.S.

Footnotes and Links: Chapter 7

(1) InternationalStudent.com. Opening a Bank Account. http://www.internationalstudent.com/international-financial-aid/opening-bank-account/
(2) Search Engine Journal, The Top 12 Online Payment Alternatives to PayPal. https://www.searchenginejournal.com/top-12-alternatives-paypal/
(3) Wikipedia. E-commerce payment systems. https://en.wikipedia.org/wiki/E-commerce_payment_system
(4) Wikipedia. *Time in the United States*. https://en.wikipedia.org/wiki/Time_in_the_United_States
(5) Wikipedia. Daylight Saving Time. https://en.wikipedia.org/wiki/Daylight_saving_time
(6) TimeandDate.com World Clock. http://www.timeanddate.com/worldclock/

C.J. SHANE

(7) Department of Homeland Security. Study in the States. Driver's License Application Process. https://studyinthestates.dhs.gov/drivers-license-application-process
(8) Craig'sList, site locator https://www.craigslist.org/about/sites
(9) Craig'sList, Avoiding Scams https://www.craigslist.org/about/scams
(10) Consumer Reports. How to Save Money When Shopping for College Textbooks. http://www.consumerreports.org/cro/news/2014/08/how-to-save-money-when-shopping-for-college-textbooks/index.htm
(11) Austin Community College. Health Insurance. *US Healthcare System Overview.*   http://www.austincc.edu/support-and-services/services-for-students/international-student-services/health-insurance
(12) U.S. Citizenship and Immigration Services. F-1 Optional Practical Training (OPT). https://www.uscis.gov/eir/visa-guide/f-1-opt-optional-practical-training/f-1-optional-practical-training-opt
(13) InternationalStudent.com. Working in the USA. http://www.internationalstudent.com/study_usa/way-of-life/working-in-the-usa/
(14) InternationalStudent.com. Working in the U.S. as an International Student. http://www.internationalstudent.com/hangouts/working-in-the-us-as-an-international-student/?autoplay=true
(15) Department of Homeland Security. Study in the States. Working in the United States. https://studyinthestates.dhs.gov/working-in-the-united-states
(16) U.S. Citizenship and Immigration Services. I-765, Application for Employment Authorization. https://www.uscis.gov/i-765
(17) Department of Homeland Security. Study in the States. Steps for Obtaining a Social Security Number. https://studyinthestates.dhs.gov/steps-for-obtaining-a-social-security-number

(18) Social Security Administration. International Students and Social Security Numbers. https://www.ssa.gov/pubs/EN-05-10181.pdf

Chapter 8. American People and Culture

The world "culture" in the English language has different meanings. For those interested in human creativity, "culture" refers to a society's achievements in the arts, philosophy, music, and literature. For scientists, the word "culture" refers to the laboratory cultivation of biological materials such as bacteria or tissue cells in an artificial medium. A third meaning is used by anthropologists and sociologists to refer to the characteristics of group of people in a select time and place. These characteristics include food, language, family and social structure, holidays and celebrations, commonly-held beliefs, customs, values, attitudes, and more.

In this chapter, we'll take the third meaning of the word and look at the culture of the United States. We'll cover some basic information about social behaviors that will help you fit more easily into the American scene.

American People

The United States is a nation of immigrants. Every American or every American's ancestors emigrated from some other place. Consequently American society is very diverse. The American population is made up of different ethnic and racial groups that represent nearly all the countries of the world.

Currently 74% of Americans are white people, mostly of European origin, but this percentage is decreasing. By 2050, white Americans of European origin will be in a minority. Currently 15% percent of Americans are Hispanic/Latino, and this percentage is increasing. Some 12% of Americans are African-American, 4.3% are Native American (this includes Alaskan natives, and native

Hawaiians). In the census records, 8% are classified as "multiracial." This last category is growing.

Example of a multiracial American: President Barak Obama

Here is an example of one well-known American - President Barack Obama. Barack Obama's mother is white of European origin, his father is black from Kenya in Africa; his half-sister (Maya Soetero Ng) shared the same white mother with Barack. Maya's father is Asian from Indonesia. Maya married a Canadian, Konrad Ng, who is ethnic Chinese. Ng's parents immigrated to Canada from Malaysia. Konrad Ng later became an American citizen.

Another example is cellist Yo-Yo Ma, born in 1955 in France to Chinese parents who immigrated to France from China in 1936. When Yo-Yo Ma was four years old, he and his family immigrated to the United States. Later Ma became a U.S. citizen. Ma married a woman of European ancestry, Jill Horner. They have two children, Nicholas and Emily.

Some Facts About Americans

Approximately 70% of Americans live in urban areas. The majority of Americans live on or near a coast. Americans move around a lot. About 20% of Americans change their residence in any one year. Eleven percent of Americans were born in another country. Of that 11%, nearly 52% were born in Latin America and 26.4% were born in Asia.

Any person born on American soil is automatically considered a legal citizen of the U.S. Immigrants can become **naturalized citizens** by learning English and passing a citizenship test. Race, religion, and ethnicity are not factors in citizenship. Anyone who becomes a naturalized citizen has the same political rights as a native-born American citizen.

For many years, 90% of Americans had a religious preference, probably because early in America's history, many immigrants came to America to flee religious persecution in Europe. However, this is changing. Each year fewer Americans express a religious preference. Religious groups in the U.S. are: Protestant Christian (50%); Catholic Christian (24%); other Christians (10%); Jewish (2%); Muslim, Hindu, or Buddhist 4%; and 10% have no religious preference.

English is the national language of the U.S. However there are areas where other languages are commonly heard. For example, in the American Southwest, Spanish is a commonly heard language as are Native American languages. Mandarin Chinese is heard often in cities like San Francisco and New York City. The most commonly spoken languages in the U.S. are English, Spanish, Chinese, Tagalog, Vietnamese, French, Korean, and German.

Marriage, Divorce, Family Life

In recent years, the number of Americans over the age of 18 who are married has declined. In 1950, only 22% of Americans were single (not married). Today, 50.2% of Americans are not married, and that number is increasing. Although there are many opportunities online and off-line to meet people, many in the younger Millennial Generation are delaying marriage or foregoing it completely.

The divorce rate in the U.S. was highest in the 1970s (23 divorces per 1,000 couples). In recent years, the divorce rate has declined to fewer than 17 divorces per 1,000 couples. Sixty-three percent of American women with children work in jobs outside the home. Between 20% and 30% of Americans now care for an elderly relative. Over time, the number of people in a typical American family has gone down. In 2015, there was an average of 3.14 persons in each American family.

There are many customs and traditions that accompany American family life. American multi-generational families often gather to eat meals together, especially on holidays. Many American families have a family pet, most often a dog or cat.

Leisure Activities, Food, Sports

Americans rank these leisure activities from most important to least important: reading, spending time with family, watching TV, fishing, going to the movies, socializing with friends and neighbors, playing team sports, exercising, gardening, participating in church activities, watching sports, computer activities, and eating out.

Because of the American population diversity, food preferences are also very diverse and represent many different ethnic groups and historical trends. Americans prefer ethnic foods in these percentages: Italian 36%, Chinese 23%, Mexican 20%, French 8%, German 6%, and Greek 2%.

People around the world often think of fast food like McDonalds and KFC as typically "American food." In fact, different regions of the U.S have different cuisines to explore. Food from the American South (states in the southeastern region) is known as "comfort food." Dishes include fried chicken, sweet potato pie, collard greens and cornbread. Near the coast, seafood dishes like shrimp are popular.

111

States in America's southwestern region were once a part of Mexico, and Mexican cuisine has great influence. In Texas, this cuisine is known as Tex-Mex, and in Arizona, as Sonoran cuisine named after the northern Mexican state of Sonora. Popular dishes are tacos and burritos. In the Pacific Northwest, salmon dishes are popular, as are different brews of coffee.

Ask Americans near your community college about the traditional foods in your region. Then try some experimentation. You may like what you try!

There are some dishes that are considered truly American such as pumpkin pie - a favorite dessert traditionally eaten at Thanksgiving dinners all over America.

Sports are very popular in the U.S. Spectator sports include national-level professional teams and collegiate teams in sports such as football, basketball, and baseball. Americans also like participatory sports that include local team sports like the ones just mentioned. Many Americans also like hiking, bicycling, swimming, and snow skiing or snowboarding.

Holidays

The U.S. federal government designates some holidays as official federal holidays. On these holidays, government offices, post offices, and banks close for the day. Examples of official holidays are: New Year's Day (January 1), Independence Day (July 4); and Thanksgiving Day (November 24).

Because of a long-standing interest in religion, many Americans observe religious holidays. Christmas, celebrated December 25, is a Christian holiday that has become something of a tradition for people of all backgrounds. Typically children get a two-week, mid-winter vacation from school to celebrate Christmas and New Year's Day.

There are other holidays that are traditional and often linked to a specific ethnic group. St. Patrick's Day is a holiday celebrated especially by Americans whose families originated from Ireland. Halloween is a nationwide that came from the ancient Celtic culture in what is now Great Britain. Halloween is celebrated nation-wide in the United States. In the Southwest, there is a closely related holiday, Día de los Muertos, that is celebrated a few days after Halloween.

American Independence Day is often simply referred to as "the Fourth of July." This major national holiday celebrates the founding of the United States and its independence from Great Britain in 1776. The holiday is celebrated with family picnics, parades, and fireworks.

Your college will maintain a calendar to inform you of federally designated and college holidays when you will have no classes.

Fireworks in Washington, D.C. on the Fourth of July

American Values

Americans do not look to historical or cultural traditions, or religious or racial identities to define us as Americans. Instead, we look to a common set of shared values based on our political rights as defined in the U.S. Constitution, and on the ideas of freedom, equal opportunity and the right to pursue the **American Dream**. These ideals regarding political rights, referred to as **civil liberties**, and economic opportunity are the primary reasons why immigrants continue to come to the United States.

Individual freedom is the most basic and fundamental American value. What do Americans mean by "freedom?" To Americans, individual freedom is "the desire and right of all individuals to control their own destiny without interference from government, a nobility class, church officials or other authorities. "(1) Americans value individuality, and encourage independent action and thought.

In return for freedom, Americans are expected to be self-reliant and independent. Our frontier heritage has created in Americans values for freedom and self-reliance.

Equality of opportunity does not mean that everyone is equal. It means that each person has an equal chance at success if that person is willing to work hard, and to prevail over the competition.

Hard work and self-discipline are values that Americans believe will lead to material success. Improving one's standard of living is often called achieving the "**American Dream**." The "Good Life" is another term Americans use to describe what Americans seek. The concepts of the American Dream and the Good Life have changed over time.

Other American values include the belief in self-improvement and a value for helping others. Americans work to improve all aspects of their lives in sports, in finances, in parenting and home life, in development of specific skills, and more. Self-improvement also includes the idea of helping others. Americans are very involved in charitable and volunteer work. The American Dream includes not only material success, but also the idea that we have a responsibility to contribute to the common good. We believe that a good life includes contributing to our community, to the nation, and to the world.

American Culture

Because America is so diverse, and because there is a great emphasis on equal opportunity among American citizens, you will meet all kinds of people while living and studying in the U.S. Please gracefully accept the assistance of workers in college, government, and business offices. Do not expect to be helped only by a person of your same race or gender.

Make eye contact when speaking to an American. A person who does not make eye contact is considered extremely shy, or worse, dishonest. Americans like some personal space, too. It's best not to stand too close to an American until you know him well. At least two feet is a good distance.

Shaking hands is most appropriate when you first meet someone or if you don't know them well. However, Americans often greet friends with a brief hug and even a kiss. A typical greeting in America is, "How are you?" Americans expect a brief answer, not a long speech about your life.

Dress and Personal Hygiene

Americans tend to be more casual in their dress than in some countries. Residents of locations with warmer weather are often very casual and wear shorts and sandals most of the time. Dressing more formally is important for job interviews, or for an important social function such as a wedding or a funeral.

Hygiene is important to most Americans. You are expected to bathe each day, keep your hair clean, use underarm deodorant, and brush your teeth regularly. Americans are sensitive to body odor, and anyone with a strong body odor is automatically unpopular.

Personal and Social Behaviors

Conversation with Americans can be a pleasurable experience, and you can learn a lot, too. Americans like to share personal stories in conversations, and they also like to make jokes and humorous remarks. You may be asked in conversation, "What do you do?" This is the common way of asking what job you have now. An appropriate answer is, "I'm a student." Also there are conversation topics that you should avoid. Americans consider it an invasion of their privacy to be asked personal questions such as how much money they make each year, what their religion is, or even how old they are. Americans are very sensitive about their weight so never ask an American how much he/she weighs or what size of dress or suit she or he wears. You should also be careful about discussion of politics.

Making insulting or discriminatory remarks about another person's religion, race, ethnicity, or gender is unacceptable. These remarks can even be seen as a hate crime, depending on how vicious the remarks are. It is also illegal to hit someone. That includes your children and your wife or husband.

Safety is an important consideration in many places in the United States. Women especially should never go alone with a stranger. It's best to take a friend with you.

Gifts can be given as a sign of appreciation to individuals who assist you to adjust to life in the United States. Gifts should be small and of moderate value. A handcrafted item or book from your home country makes a good gift. Americans typically open wrapped gifts immediately and expect you to open a gift when they give it to you. Do not expect to receive favors or gifts in return for your gift giving.

Bribery is illegal in the United States. You cannot legally give money, valuables, or favors to anyone in exchange for benefits to you. For example, it is illegal to bribe a professor for a higher grade, or to bribe a police officer to avoid a traffic ticket, etc. Even attempting to bribe someone can lead to your arrest.

Academic Behavior:

Americans have strict rules and guidelines about proper academic behavior. You are expected to always do your own work. You cannot do homework or take tests for another student, nor can that student do your homework or take tests for you.

You must be very careful not to copy passages from others' works or research findings without attributing the passages to the author. In your essays, you may quote a passage from another work, or you may quote research findings. However, you must indicate in a footnote where you found the material. Including passages as if you wrote them yourself is called **plagiarism**. It is an offense that can lead to your dismissal as a student and the end of your academic career.

The website *A Research Guide for Students* has good guidelines on how to avoid plagiarism. Also talk to your professor if you have a question about this important topic. (2) Another good source on avoiding plagiarism is *WriteCheck*, 6 Ways to Avoid Plagiarism in Research Papers. (3)

Culture Shock

A very common problem that international students will experience is culture shock. This is a sense of disorientation caused by living in the United States, feelings of constant stress and frustration, anxiety, loneliness, mental depression, and sometimes physical symptoms such as pain and inability to sleep. This is often accompanied by an extreme longing for your home and family.

Everyone misses home, but you may find that missing home becomes so strong it is difficult to concentrate on your school work, or to enjoy anything in your life. Culture shock is normal. Americans also experience culture shock when they go to live, work, or study in another country. Then when they return to the U.S., they have a period of adjustment called "reverse culture shock." That may happen to you, too!

There are several strategies to help you deal with what is a very normal response to a huge life change – leaving home and moving to a very different culture. Try these strategies:

- maintain contact with your family and friends at home, and if you are a religious person, visit a local church, mosque, temple, or synagogue;
- make contact with other students from your home country, create opportunities to speak your own language, and even have a traditional meal together;
- get involved in a student club or organization geared toward your own personal interests. Perhaps you are interested in sports or photography or becoming a teacher or learning how to design a website or exploring hiking and bicycling trails. Get to know both international students and American students in the club and participate in club activities.

Overcoming Loneliness and Culture Shock

Most community colleges have a **counseling** service for students to visit and seek help with different kinds of problems, including culture shock. Americans are accustomed to seeking help at a counseling center, but this may be a new experience for you as an international student. At the counseling center, you will get an opportunity to talk about your feelings, and get assistance with strategies for dealing with culture shock.

InternationalStudent.com has some great idea about how to deal with culture shock, including two videos from Columbia University in New York. (4) The presenter, Dan Fishel, makes us laugh as he describes the phases of his own culture shock, and how he overcame it. He talks about culture shock as the experience of living in a fog, or walking through a cloud. He found his way out the fog, and you can, too!

~~~

In our next section, we'll learn about some community colleges in different areas of the United States. By reading these college profiles, you will get some ideas about what to consider when choosing a college, and what questions to ask to help you decide.

Footnotes and Links: Chapter 8

(1). Maryanne Kearny Datesman, JoAnn Crandall, Edward N. Kearney, "Traditional American Values and Beliefs," in *American Ways: An Introduction to American Culture,* 3rd ed., Pearson Education, 2005.
(2) A Research Guide for Students. Plagiarism: How to Avoid It. http://www.aresearchguide.com/6plagiar.html
(3) WriteCheck.com. 6 Ways to Avoid Plagiarism in Research Papers. http://en.writecheck.com/ways-to-avoid-plagiarism/

(4) InternationalStudent.com Culture Shock.
http://www.internationalstudent.com/study_usa/way-of-life/culture-shock/

Chapter 9. Profiles of Community Colleges

As mentioned in chapter 2, there are several things to think about when choosing a community college. Your academic and career goals are a fundamental consideration. You want a college that will prepare you to achieve these goals. Does the community college have the services you need? Can you find tutoring to help you with your classes? Are there intensive ESL classes to help you improve your English?

Transfer options are a key consideration when choosing a community college. Let's imagine that you already have your mind set on studying at a specific four-year university because it has an academic degree program that meets your career goals. That means your path will be eased if you choose a community college that has a transfer agreement with the four-year university of your choice.

Academic goals aside, keep in mind that you are embarking on a great adventure by studying in the U.S. You will have personal goals as well as academic goals. Let's imagine that you want to live in a city with a diverse culture. Or perhaps you want to live in a place where you can participate in outdoor sporting events or to regularly attend major athletic events. Perhaps climate and weather are considerations. You love snowy mountains where you can ski and snowboard. Or maybe you prefer hot weather and swimming in the ocean.

Money is always a consideration. If you don't have a lot of money, you will want to choose a location where the overall cost of living is lower. You can save a lot of money if you live in a city where the monthly apartment rent is $500 rather than $1,000 each month.

A great resource to determine cost of living is the website Numbeo.com/cost-of-living/. You can search for the costs of food, housing, restaurant meals, cinema tickets, etc. in cities across the United States, and worldwide, too. The Numbeo cost of living index uses New York City as the basis for calculations. The New York City cost of living index is 100%. This means that if a city is 75%, then the cost of living is 75% of New York City. The index does not include apartment rental fees. Rental fees are listed separately.

In the following pages, we look at seven community colleges located in very different areas of the U.S. Each college has its own attributes and strengths. Look at the categories of information in these profiles such as academics, services offered to students, tuition costs, housing and cost of living, and what kinds of test scores you must submit to be admitted into the college. Then apply these same categories to any community college that interests you.

Name of College: **Austin Community College**
Location: Austin, Texas
College Website URL: http://www.austincc.edu/
International Student Page:
http://www.austincc.edu/apply-and-register/type-of-student/international-admission-steps

Introduction

Austin Community College is a public educational institution in Austin, Texas. The college has 11 campuses and additional centers in the Austin metropolitan area and nearby towns. The two largest campus branches are El Rio and Riverside. Students can earn an associate degree or certificate in more than 100 different areas. The student-faculty ratio is 21 to 1 (21 students to each faculty member).

Currently there are 361 international students with F-1 visas attending Austin CC, and an addition 155 with other visa categories. The international student centers are at the Riverside and Round Rock campuses. International students can take classes at more than one campus. The majority of international students take classes at Rio Grande, Riverside, and Northridge campuses. Countries sending the greatest number of international students to Austin CC are South Korea, India, Vietnam, Mexico, and China. The most popular degree programs for international students are business, international business, and engineering.

Rio Grande Campus, Austin Community College, Austin, Texas

Academic Programs

Austin Community College (ACC) offers more than one type of academic program. The first is the associate degree designed for students who intend to transfer to a four-year college or university and earn a bachelor's degree. Students take core courses that will transfer to the four-year university, as well as introductory classes in the student's major course of study.

ACC also offers an associate degree in applied science for individuals who plan to seek employment immediately after receiving this degree. Examples of these career and technical degrees include business and technical communications, emergency medical services, paralegal studies, and travel and tourism.

A full range of English-language learning options are available at Austin Community College. These programs help students to speak better everyday conversational English, and to improve English needed in academic coursework. The college offers an Intensive English Program for those students primarily interested in focusing on English-language skills.

Services Offered

Austin Community College requires that international students attend a mandatory orientation before classes begin. The college offers extensive advising services to help students make the best academic decisions in their major. If a student is not sure what s/he wants to major in, Austin CC can help with exploring majors and careers. A Career Services Center helps students with career development. Counseling services help students deal with personal and career issues as well.

Austin CC provides required college and course readiness assessment tests to help students enroll in the best classes for his/her proficiency level. This includes English-language assessments. Austin CC also offers students both a learning lab and tutoring options.

International Students Services helps students with a wide variety of issues including academic advising, maintaining their visa, travel outside the U.S., required forms, and more. The college also advises international students on housing questions, driver's license requirements, health insurance needs, and public transportation options.

Also available are activities to help students engage and improve their quality of experience. These include community service opportunities, student organizations, student media and student government, as well as special events and activities.

Test Scores

Austin Community College requires international students whose native language is not English to take an English proficiency test. Scores must be either TOEFL or IELTS. Austin CC's website tells us, "A TOEFL score of 550 (paper-based test) or 79 (online test), or an Academic IELTS overall band score of 6.5 required for admissions with the F-1, F-2, J-1, and J-2 visa types."

Austin CC also has minimum educational requirements depending on the country of origin. For example, Brazilian students are required to have earned the Diploma/Certificado de Ensino Médio. South Korean students must have earned the Senior High School Diploma. There is a long list of countries with requirements here:

Minimum Education Requirements.

http://www.austincc.edu/apply-and-register/type-of-student/international-admission-steps/minimum-admission-requirements

Tuition and Cost:

Tuition and fees for out-of-state and international students is $1,134 for a three-credit course. Austin CC estimates that an international student will need $25,000 to cover an academic year (nine months). This includes tuition and fees, living expenses, etc.

Top Transfer Schools

Austin Community College offers a transfer core curriculum that is designed to transfer to a four-year college for the purpose of earning a bachelor's degree. The college offers transfer services, including advising and counseling, and a Transfer Academy that helps students with a transfer planning guide and workshops aimed at a successful transfer.

Austin CC has an impressive list of transfer relationships with colleges in Texas and around the United States. Among Austin CC's top transfer schools is the University of Texas at Austin. UT Austin is ranked number 16 overall nationally for public institutions, number seven for undergraduate programs for business and number 11 for undergraduate programs in engineering. Texas State University in nearby San Marcos, Texas, is also a top transfer university for Austin CC students.

Housing and Cost of Living

International students typically live in apartments in Austin while attending Austin Community College, because the college does not provide student housing. The college does provide information on locating an apartment and on rental leases. Apartments in Austin range from $968 for a one-bedroom apartment outside the city center to $1,447 in the city center. The cost-of-living index for Austin excluding rents is 69.10. For more specifics on Austin's cost of living, go to Numbeo.com

About the Location

Austin, Texas, home of Austin Community College, is the capital of the state of Texas. The city is located in central Texas on the Colorado River. Austin has a population of nearly 1 million, and the metro area, including Round Rock, has a population of over 2 million. The city is historically important. Texas was originally the home of several Native Americans tribes. Texas became a part of the Spanish empire. Then after Mexican independence, Texas became a part of Mexico. In 1836, Texas rebelled against Mexican rule and became an independent nation for 10 years. Austin was the capital of the Republic of Texas, then continued as state capital when Texas joined the United States in 1846.

As well as being the center of Texas government, Austin is an important educational center with several colleges and universities, chief among them the University of Texas at Austin. The city has a wide variety of cultural opportunities throughout the year including museums, and film, theater and cultural festivals.

Music is a key factor in Austin's cultural life. In fact, the official slogan of the city is, "The Live Music Capital of the

World." Austin has numerous music festivals including the Austin City Limits Music Festival, the Old Settlers' Music Festival, and the internationally famous South By Southwest, a set of music and film festivals, conferences, and other events. The city has numerous music venues - concert halls, restaurants, bars, and nightclubs - where residents can hear music day and night.

Austin is considered a humid subtropical climate with hot, humid summers, and mild winter days with cool winter nights. Snow in Austin is not common. Because of the mild climate, outdoor activities are common. Among these outdoor activities are bicycling, hiking, and boating on the Colorado River.

The official website for the city of Austin is http://www.austintexas.gov/ and you can learn more here: http://www.austintexas.org/visit/

Name of College: Bunker Hill Community College
Location: Boston, Massachusetts
College Website URL: http://www.bhcc.mass.edu/
International Student Pages:
admissions:
http://www.bhcc.mass.edu/internationalcenter/international forms/
international center:
http://www.bhcc.mass.edu/internationalcenter/

Introduction
Bunker Hill Community College is the largest community college in the state of Massachusetts. It is a public-funded community college with an open-admissions policy. Approximately 14,000 students attend Bunker Hill. The average age of Bunker Hill students is 26. The majority of all students attend college part-time. Fifty-seven percent of the students are women. The student body is

diverse: blacks/African-Americans are 24%; whites are 25%, Hispanics 24%, and Asians 10%.

The college has two campuses - Chelsea and Charlestown – and three satellite locations. The Charlestown campus is where we find most of the international students. The 952 international students come from 101 different countries. The top five countries represented at Bunker Hill CC are China, Vietnam, South Korea, Japan, and Morocco. The most popular fields of study for international students are engineering, business, and computer science.

Academic Programs

Bunker Hill CC offers over 100 associate degrees and certificates in arts and sciences. The college also provides Optional Practical Training (OPT) programs for international students. Class size is small at Bunker Hill CC, only 20 students for each professor.

In addition to associate degree programs, Bunker Hill CC offers certificates in such academic programs information technology security, computed tomography, and practical nursing.

Services Offered

Bunker Hill CC provides numerous support services for international students. The International Center on the Charlestown campus aims to be a "home away from home" for international students. The International Center provides orientation programs for new students, advice and counseling on housing, immigration issues, and academic and personal matters. In addition to these services, international students can also take advantage of services provided to all Bunker Hill Community College students. These include free tutoring, an on-campus health center, and the LifeMap program which helps students to plan and achieve educational and personal goals. Bunker Hill provides extensive support in English as a Second Language (ESL), including the "paired courses" program in which students combine an academic course with ESL support.

Test Scores

International students must prove English-language proficiency. If students are already in the U.S., they can take the BHCC Placement Test. If the student is still living in his/her home country, then the TOEFL test or the IELTS test is required. TOEFL written score must be at least 423, and at least 38 on the TOEFL iBT. Students must earn a score of at least 5 on the IELTS. Students not meeting the language proficiency requirement may receive conditional acceptance into Bunker Hill CC. They will then enroll in EC Boston Language School and study English until their skill level is higher.

Tuition and Costs

The current non-resident tuition fee for one credit hour is $128; for a three-credit course, tuition is $384. Bunker Hill Community College provides an estimated budget for International Students here: http://www.bhcc.edu/media/03-documents/Budget.pdf

Top Transfer Schools

Bunker Hill CC has articulation agreements (transfer agreements) with a lengthy list of private and public colleges and universities available for viewing on the college website. Note that Bunker Hill CC participates in the MassTransfer program that facilitates transfer to a number of universities and colleges in the state of Massachusetts. MassTransfer is a project of the Massachusetts Department of Higher Education. Learn more about MassTransfer at www.mass.edu/masstransfer/

Housing and Cost of Living

Bunker Hill CC does not provide on-campus housing. Most international students share an apartment with other students. Living away from the city center is less expensive and students are advised to use public transportation to travel to their campus.

Average cost for a one-bedroom apartment range from $1,531 (away from city center) to $2,276 (city center). The cost-of-living index for Boston is 83.91. Go to Numbeo.com for specifics on the cost of living excluding rents in Boston. The Practical Matters page on Bunker Hill's International Center web page has information on finding rental property.

About the Location

Boston is the largest city and capital of Massachusetts. It is located in the northeast of the United States on the Atlantic coast. Boston is one of America's oldest cities and the site of many important historical events. It was founded by English Puritan immigrants in 1630. The city was an important center of revolutionary activity in the era in which America revolted against the British Empire and declared independence in 1776.

The greater Boston area includes several well-known smaller cities such as Cambridge, Charlestown, Chelsea, Quincy and Watertown. The Charles River divides Boston from some of these smaller cities.

As an internationally recognized center of higher education, greater Boston is the home to a long list of well-known educational institutions. Among them are Harvard University and Massachusetts Institute of Technology (MIT). Boston has long been viewed as an important center of business and technological innovation. Boston's numerous cultural opportunities include museums, music festivals, and historical-event commemorations. The city is the home of several professional sports teams, including the Boston Red Sox (baseball) and Boston Celtics (basketball). An important sports event is the annual Boston Marathon.

Public transport is well-developed in Boston. The city has a subway system, and the Bunker Hill Community College Charlestown campus has its own subway stop that is only 10 minutes from downtown Boston. Boston has a high cost of living compared to many American cities.

Boston has a humid climate with cold, rainy and often snowy winters, and warm-to-hot and humid summers. The nearby Atlantic Ocean has an effect on Boston's weather. Sea breezes and fogs are common, and tropical storms and hurricanes occur from time to time.

The city's website is: http://www.cityofboston.gov/ and more information is here: http://www.visitboston.org/

Name of College: Cabrillo College
Location: Aptos, California (near Santa Cruz, CA)
College Website URL: http://www.cabrillo.edu/
International Student page:
https://www.cabrillo.edu/services/international/

Introduction

Cabrillo College is a two-year public community college located in Aptos, California, on the Pacific Coast at Monterey Bay. Aptos is considered a suburb of the larger city of Santa Cruz, California. Over 15,000 students attend Cabrillo College. There are two Cabrillo campuses: one at Aptos, and the second at Watsonville about ten miles south of Aptos. Although international students can take classes at both campuses, most of the international students are found on the Aptos campus. The teacher-student ratio is one teacher to 25 students. Cabrillo is an open-admissions college.

Nearly 75% of all Cabrillo students are under the age of 30. Female students make up nearly 55% of the student body, and males almost 45%. Nearly 45% of Cabrillo students attend college full-time, and nearly 55% are part-time students. Almost 40% of Cabrillo students are of Hispanic/Latino ethnicity. The college is a federally-designated Hispanic-serving educational institution.

In late 2016, there were 70 international students at Cabrillo College from 35 different countries. The top five countries sending students to Cabrillo were China, South Korea, Japan, France, and Brazil. The most popular fields of study for international students at Cabrillo are business, psychology, engineering, and accounting.

The college has an innovative sustainability program that includes campus water and energy conservation projects.

Cabrillo College was named after the explorer Juan Rodríguez Cabrillo (b.1499-d.1543) who explored the west coast of North American for the Spanish Empire. He was the first European to explore the coast of what is now California.

Academic Programs

Cabrillo College offers two-year associate degrees with courses that are transferable to a four-year university. Cabrillo has a unique Associate Degree for Transfer (AA-T or AS-T) which guarantees transfer into the California State University system if you meet minimum academic requirements. In addition, the college has Career Technical Education (CTE) classes leading to certificates in specialized employment areas.

Cabrillo College also offers on-line classes called "distance education." Eight online degrees are offered. You can take more than 50 different courses online that meet the general education requirement.

Services Offered

Cabrillo College offers a wide range of services to students to create a positive college experience. Students can receive both academic and personal counseling. Services are available for disabled students, including assistive technology, for students with learning disabilities, for educationally and economically disadvantaged students, for Latino students, and for military veterans.

Cabrillo's Learning Communities Center gives you an opportunity to join a community organized around a "theme" that interests you. You will take classes on that theme, meet new friends with similar interests, and work together as a cohort group. Learning communities include business, and math and science themes.

Cabrillo College, Aptos, California

The college has a required on-line orientation program for first-time students that you will take before you register for classes. In addition to general orientation to college life, Cabrillo has two additional programs for students: Assessment and Educational Planning.

After completing the online orientation, you will go through the Assessment Process.

Assessment is required of all new students for the purpose of placing you in the right math, English and English as a Second Language class. Assessment is waived for students who can provide select required documents.

Following assessment, the next step is the Educational Planning process, a part of the orientation program that will help you plan for, and achieve your academic goals. Academic counselors will assist you in creating your Education Plan. Career counseling is also available.

Learn more about student services at Cabrillo College here: http://www.cabrillo.edu/home/services.html

Additional learning resources are available including a free tutoring center, a math center, and an English-learning center. Learn more here: https://www.cabrillo.edu/home/learning.html

Test Scores

Cabrillo College requires a TOEFL score of 480/54 (480 on pBT, 157 on cBT, or 54 on iBT). IELTS scores of 5.5 or higher are accepted. If you scores are not sufficiently high for immediate entry, you can participate in an Intensive English Program. One example of an intensive program is the Middlebury Institute of International Studies at Monterey (California) located south of the Cabrillo campus. Intensive English Programs are not the same as a Cabrillo College English as a Second Language (ESL) academic courses leading to an associate degree in ESL.

Tuition/Costs

For six units of academic credit, international students pay $1,530 for tuition and an additional $75 in fees (health services, transportation, etc.). The total for six units is $1,605. More information can be found at https://www.cabrillo.edu/services/ar/fees-fallspring.html

Top Transfer Schools

California universities are the most important transfer schools for Cabrillo international students. Many transfer to University of California system universities such as UC Santa Cruz, UC Davis, and UC Berkeley. Also important are California State University universities such as California State University at Monterey Bay, San Jose State University, and San Francisco State University.

As mentioned earlier, Cabrillo has an Associate Degree for Transfer (AA-T or AS-T) which guarantees transfer into the California State University system if a student meets minimum academic requirements. The program includes 23 degree programs with more in development. Learn more at Cabrillo's Transfer Center. https://www.cabrillo.edu/services/transfercenter/

Housing/Cost of Living

Cabrillo College does not provide on-campus student housing. The college does provide information and resources to help students find housing.

Cabrillo recommends that new students stay with a home-stay family for the first semester. This will give you an opportunity to learn more about the housing situation and to find something that suits you. The college advises you to be very cautious about arranging housing in advance and making payments to housing agencies before you arrive in the U.S. For information about home stays and other housing options for international students, go to: https://www.cabrillo.edu/services/international/housing.html

Numbeo.com reports that the cost-of-living index, including rent, for nearby Santa Cruz, California, is 76.95. Rent per month for a one-bedroom apartment in Santa Cruz is $1,685 per month in the city center, and $1,411.11 outside the city center.

About the Location

Cabrillo College is located in Aptos, California, in Santa Cruz County, quite close to the city of Santa Cruz.

Beautiful Monterey Bay on the Pacific Coast is just a short distance from the Cabrillo campus. There are numerous opportunities for beach activities, including the Santa Cruz Beach Boardwalk. Wooded mountains complete the lovely scenery.

Nearby are natural areas, trails for hiking and biking, and even the yearly Monarch Butterfly Annual Migration watch at Natural

Bridges State Beach. At Año Nuevo Natural Preserve north of Santa Cruz, you can watch elephant seals year-round. Just south of Aptos is the world famous Monterey Bay Aquarium and Monterey Bay National Marine Sanctuary.

Arts and culture events abound, and there are several arts centers and arts galleries. The region has an Artists' Open Studios event every fall.

For foodies, there's the Santa Cruz Chocolate Festival. And this region of California has numerous wineries and farmer's markets, too.

A resource guide for Aptos, California, can be found here: http://www.aptos.ca/ and more information is here: http://www.santacruz.org/

Name of College: **Colorado Mountain College**
Location: Colorado (Steamboat Springs, Leadville, Spring Valley, etc.)
College Website URL: http://coloradomtn.edu/
International Student Page:
http://coloradomtn.edu/admissions/international_students/

Introduction

Colorado Mountain College (CMC) is a highly-ranked American college with some special aspects that make it unique among American community colleges. Colorado Mountain College has three residential campuses and eight community campuses located in the small towns in the Rocky Mountains. The territory covered by Colorado Mountain College includes most of Colorado's major ski resorts as well as three national forests and six wilderness areas. All international students study at one of CMC's residential campuses: Steamboat Springs, Leadville, or Spring Valley (between Glenwood Springs and Carbondale) with some occasional exceptions at the Edwards campus. The community campuses include Aspen, Breckenridge, Dillon, Carbondale, Buena Vista, Edwards, Glenwood Springs, and Rifle, Colorado.

CMC offers a full range of two-year associate degrees and one-semester certification programs in several academic and professional areas. In recent years, the college began offering bachelor degrees in five academic fields. The student-to-professor ratio is 12 to one.

Currently Colorado Mountain has 33 international students. The college is actively working now to actively recruit more international students.

Colorado Mountain College

Academic Programs

Colorado Mountain College offers a full range of associate degree programs in areas such as accounting, entrepreneurship, environmental science, outdoor education, resort management, and art. Certificate programs cover some traditional areas such as computer technology and accounting/bookkeeping as well as programs that are not often seen at American community colleges. These include Ski & Snowboard Business and Wilderness Medical Emergency Services.

An innovative program at Colorado Mountain College is the Isaacson School of New Media which offers studies in digital media, professional photography, graphic design, and fusion workshops that keep students up-to-date with digital technology.

Beginning in 2012, CMC began offering bachelor degree programs in two areas: Business Administration and Sustainability Studies. Three additional bachelor degrees have since been added: Elementary Education, Leadership and Management, and Nursing.

Services Offered

Colorado Mountain College provides a required orientation for new residential students at each of the three residential campuses: Leadville, Steamboat Springs, and Spring Valley. The college also offers myCMCSuccess Online orientation.

Additional services for students include student academic advising, personal counseling, tutoring, IT service desk help with technology problems, career services, and college library services.

The college offers assessment testing services for degree-seeking and certificate-seeking students. ACT, SAT, and Accuplacer scores are used as assessment tools. If a student has not taken the ACT or SAT test, s/he will be assessed with Accuplacer in order to be placed in the correct classes. The college offers a range of services for disabled students as well.

Test Scores

International students must prove English-language proficiency at the time of admission in order to receive the I-20 form required for a student visa. Proficiency can be proven by submitting test scores at the time of admission. Minimum scores are: TOEFL-61 or higher on the iBT, or 500 or higher on the written test; Michigan Test of English Language Proficiency--80 or higher; International English Language Testing Service (IELTS) test- 6.5, with no band below a 6; or advanced-level completion documents from one of several language schools in the U.S.

Colorado Mountain College does not offer an intensive program in English as a Second Language.

Tuition/Costs

Out-of-state students pay $ 429 per credit hour for lower-level courses. Total costs to attend Colorado Mountain College (tuition, fees, housing, books, supplies, etc.) for an out-of-state resident for nine months (two semesters) are estimated as $23,518. According to CMC's website, "international students can apply for CMC scholarships that have no 'residency' requirement, prior to the March 1 deadline, but these can provide only limited assistance."

Top Transfer Schools

The Colorado Mountain College website has a lengthy list of public and private universities which have accepted CMC graduates into their four-year bachelor programs, including several Ivy League schools. CMC participates in the Guaranteed General Education Project. This program guarantees credit transfers to public colleges and universities in the state of Colorado.

Housing/Cost of Living

International students live in residential halls at one of three campuses: Leadville, Spring Valley or Steamboat Springs. Each room has a private bath. These costs are $2,361 per semester for a double room (two students in a room) or $3,361 for a single room. The residential halls have a dining hall with meal plan available as well as a campus café. In most cases, international students are required to live in CMC's on-campus housing. Numbeo.com does not have cost-of-living data on these small towns in Colorado.

About the Location

Because Colorado Mountain College is located in the Rocky Mountains of north-central Colorado, the ecology, scenery, and recreational activities are unique. Snowy winters and cool summers attract thousands of tourists for both seasons. CMC students have an excellent opportunity to participate in activities such as mountain biking, camping, kayaking and rafting, hiking, fishing, hot-air ballooning, horseback riding, skiing and snowboarding. In fact, eight Colorado Mountain College student athletes participated in the 2014 Olympics in Sochi, Russia.

The towns with CMC campuses are all small. The populations of the three CMC residential campus towns are: Steamboat Springs, 12,088; Leadville, 2,580; and Glenwood Springs/Spring Valley, approximately 10,000. They share small-town advantages such as clean air, and opportunities to meet and know neighbors. Individual towns have special attractions. For example, Glenwood Springs has a large outdoor mineral hot springs pool. Colorado Mountain College has some distinctive attractions, both academic and recreational, for international students.

A guide to Glenwood Springs, Colorado, is found at
http://www.visitglenwood.com/
and to northwest Colorado at
http://www.colorado.com/northwest

Name of College: **Pima Community College**
Location: Tucson, Arizona
College Website URL: https://www.pima.edu/index.html
International Student page: https://pima.edu/new-students/international/index.html

Introduction

Pima Community College is a public educational institution with approximately 44,000 credit-seeking students. The college has six campuses in the Tucson metropolitan area, as well as education centers for additional locations. The two largest campuses with the greatest number of students are West Campus and Downtown Campus. The average age of Pima CC students is 27. Part-time students make up 68% of the student body; 32% are full-time students. The college has an open admissions policy, does not charge an application fee, and follows a semester academic calendar. The student faculty ratio is 25 to 1.

In 2016, Pima Community College had 207 international students and additional international students in Optional Practical Training (OPT) programs. Currently, Pima Community College has a growing international program with a strong recruitment effort. The college is eager to receive more international students. The top five countries sending students to Pima Community College are: China, Mexico, Saudi Arabia, Vietnam, and Korea. Business and engineering are the most popular programs for international students at Pima Community College. Pima CC is a member of the Hispanic Association of Colleges and Universities (HACU), and as such, is committed to Hispanic higher education success.

Academic programs

Pima Community College offers international students the 2 + 2 option. You can earn two degrees: a two-year associate degree, and then transfer to a four-year college or university and earn a bachelor's degree in two additional years. Currently Pima CC has 185 transfer and occupational programs. Pima CC offers students the opportunity to earn associate degrees in arts (AA); in business administration (ABUS); in fine arts (AFA); and in science (AS). Credits earned in these degree programs are transferrable to a four-year college. The college also has a certificate for the Arizona General Education Curriculum with courses that can be transferred as well. Pima CC offers courses for both in-classroom and online classes.

Pima CC offers students options for improving their English. For associate-degree seeking students, Pima CC offers ESL (English as a Second Language) courses in Reading, Writing, Oral Communication, Pronunciation, and American Culture. For individuals not yet enrolled in a Pima degree program but who want to improve their English, Pima offers intermediate to advanced ESL courses.

Services offered

Pima Community College has a Center for International Education and Global Engagement located on the West Campus. At this Center, students can receive immigration advising, academic advising, and assistance with adjusting to American culture. The college also has a free, mandatory New Student Orientation Program that provides academic advising and information on college life for all students

The college requires all new students (everyone, not just international students) to take assessment tests in reading, writing, and mathematics. An English proficiency test may be required depending on your TOEFL score. You will be placed in academic classes appropriate to your level based on these assessment tests. The college offers workshops to help you get ready for the assessment tests.

Pima Community College, West Campus

AMERICAN COMMUNITY COLLEGES

Test Scores

International students who plan to seek an associate degree at Pima CC are required to submit TOEFL scores. Minimum TOEFL scores are 61 internet-based test/173 computer-based test/500 paper-based test. Students with scores lower than this can be admitted to the college, but they will be required to take ESL classes to upgrade their English to college level.. IELTS, ACT, and other scores will be accepted in the summer of 2017. English test scores are waived for students from English-speaking countries, or if they can prove their high school classes were taught in English. For students who plan to start at PCC's ESL program, these test scores are not required. Upon completion of the ESL program, students can then transition to the academic programs. Upon arrival in Tucson, students must take additional assessment tests to determine English-language proficiency. They will be placed in classes appropriate to their proficiency level based upon these assessment tests.

Tuition/Costs

Pima CC has "general" and "differential" tuition rates depending on the academic program. The current general tuition (2016) for non-resident (out-of-state) students is $300 per credit hour. Learn more about calculating your tuition here: https://www.pima.edu/paying-for-school/costs/docs/tuition-calculation-worksheet.pdf

The college also provides a Net Price Calculator to help students estimate all costs including tuition, required fees, books and supplies, housing and meals, and addition expenses. https://www.pima.edu/web/net-price-calculator/npc.htm

Top Transfer Schools

Pima Community College has transfer agreements with several universities, both public and private. International students' top choices for transfer are: the University of Arizona, Arizona State University, Northern Arizona University, and Colorado State.

International students will be especially interested in in Pima CC's transfer partner, the University of Arizona, also located in Tucson. This university has several top-ranked academic programs, among them business entrepreneurship (No. 7 in the U.S.) and business management information systems (No. 4 in the U.S.); and undergraduate engineering (No. 55 in the U.S). Additional highly-ranked programs include anthropology (No. 3); sociology (No. 7), communication (No. 8), geography (No. 8), public administration (No. 11), philosophy (No. 13), linguistics (No. 14) and political science (No. 21). According to *Science Watch*, the University of Arizona is the top-ranked research U.S. university for planetary exploration and planetary research, and it has a No. 6 global ranking for space science.

Housing/Cost of Living

International students who attend Pima Community College typically live in off-campus apartments as there are no college dorms. However near Pima CC West Campus there are several student apartment complexes within walking and bicycling distance with monthly rents of $300 to $700. The monthly rental cost for a one-bedroom apartment in the city center is $612, and $560 outside the city center. The cost of living index excluding rents for Tucson is 63.59. For specifics, go to Numbeo.com.

About the Location

Pima Community College is located in Tucson, Arizona, in the American Southwest. The city is in the Sonoran Desert and is surrounded by mountains. Tucson has a population of about 500,000 with a metro area of over 1 million residents.

Tucson is a very old city. In fact, it is often referred to as the "Old Pueblo." There was a Native American settlement at Tucson for several millennia. During the Spanish colonial period, a military fort known as El Presidio San Agustín del Tucsón was established, and in 1700, Father Eusebio Kino founded the San Xavier del Bac Mission. The San Xavier mission continues to serve the local native tribe, the Tohono O'odham. San Xavier del Bac is considered the best example of baroque architecture in the United States. It is often referred to as the "White Dove of the Desert." Following Spanish colonial rule, Tucson and the surrounding area of what is now southern Arizona became part of Mexico. It then became American territory when the region was purchased by the U.S. in 1858 (Gadsden Purchase).

This history, plus the fact that Tucson is only 60 miles/97 km from the Mexican border, means that Mexican and Native Americans cultures have had -- and continue to have -- a strong influence on the culture of the city. Tucson has a large Native American and Hispanic American population. Mexican-Americans make up 36% of the city's population. Spanish is widely spoken.

The city has a vibrant cultural life. There are many internationally-known festivals and conferences. Examples are the Tucson Gem & Mineral Show (largest in the world), Tucson Festival of Books (4th largest in the U.S.), Tucson Rodeo, Tucson Meet Yourself, and the All Souls Procession which is modeled on the Mexican holiday of Dia de los Muertos. The city has many cultural sites such as museums and art galleries plus art events such as film festivals, music festivals, etc. The Arizona-Sonoran Desert Museum is considered world-class. Tucson also is a center for mariachi music.

The city has been designated a "world city of gastronomy" by UNESCO. Cuisines from around the world can be found in the Old Pueblo, as well as a number of innovative community food programs, food banks, and farmers' markets.

Tucson is a "dark sky" city which means that city ordinances have been passed to limit light pollution. Major observatories, including Kitt Peak National Observatory, can be found in the region near Tucson, and astronomers come from around the world to take advantage of the clear desert night sky.

Popular outdoor activities are hiking and bicycling. El Tour de Tucson brings in 10,000 or more bicyclists every winter for a bike race, and professional long-distance bicyclists frequently train in

Tucson. Winter skiing is an option on Mount Lemmon on the northern edge of Tucson. Saguaro National Park and its hiking trails are located in two parts on the east and west sides of the city. Tourism is a very important industry and the city is home to numerous resorts and hotels.

Tucson has a dry desert climate, with has hot summers, and a monsoon rain season that usually begins the first week of July. Spring and fall seasons are brief. Winters are mild and sunny which attracts tourists from around the world. Snowfall is the city of Tucson is quite rare. Because of its higher elevation, Tucson is cooler than the Arizona capital city of Phoenix.

Learn more about Tucson here https://www.tucsonaz.gov/ and here https://www.visittucson.org/

Name of College: Valencia College
Location: Orlando, Florida
College Website URL: http://valenciacollege.edu/
International Student Page:
http://valenciacollege.edu/international/

Introduction

Valencia College is a top-ranked American community college. In 2012, Valencia won the Aspen Prize for best community college in the U.S. Valencia had been known as Valencia Community College, but the name was changed in 2010 to Valencia College when the college began offering bachelor's degrees. Valencia College has five campuses and three service sites in the Orlando mid-Florida region. The professor-to-student ratio is 1 to 23. The student population of over 70,000 is very ethnically diverse, including 32.5% Hispanic. As such, Valencia is designated a "Hispanic serving" Institution.

In the fall of 2015, Valencia College had a total of 1,509 international students. Some were F-1 visa students studying for a degree, others were in the intensive English program, and still others participated in the Disney College Program as interns. Most international students attend classes at Valencia's West campus in southwest Orlando. The top countries contributing international students to Valencia College are Brazil, Venezuela, Saudi Arabia, Vietnam, and China. The most popular fields of study for international students are business administration, engineering, hospitality and tourism management, and architecture.

West Building at Valencia College, Orlando, Florida

Academic Programs

Valencia College today offers over 100 programs leading to associate degrees and certificates, plus bachelor's degrees in a limited number of fields. The most popular program is the General Studies program which provides a basic liberal arts education, and is equivalent to the first two years at a university. The college provides plans for transferring coursework to a four-year university.

Valencia also offers associate degree and certificate programs in several areas, among them arts/entertainment, business, communications, education, engineering/computer programming, health sciences, hospitality/tourism and more. A unique program offered in the arts/entertainment area is an Associate of Science degree in Film Production Technology that has been described by film director Steven Spielberg as "one of the best film schools in the country."

Two English-language learning programs are available at Valencia College. The year-round Intensive English Program is for beginner through advanced students who are age 15 and up. This program also provides assistance for transferring to Valencia College as a degree-seeking student. In the summer, the ESL for Teens program takes students ages 12 through 15.

Services Offered

Valencia College's International Student Services assist international students in a number of areas including academic, immigration and personal counseling. Free tutoring services are available to students. The college has a library on each campus available to international students. Also available are free Wi-Fi and on-campus computer labs, plus the Atlas program, an on-line learning community.

Test Scores

Valencia College requires proof of English-language proficiency unless the student comes from a country on the English-proficiency waiver list. TOEFL scores must be a minimum of 45, IELTS scores must be a minimum of 5.5, or a minimum of 40 on the COMPASS ESL assessment test.

Tuition/Costs

Out-of-state/non-residents pay $390.96 per credit hour for an associate degree program, and $427.59 per credit hour for a bachelor's degree program. The total estimated cost for international students to attend Valencia College for one year is $24,904. This includes tuition/fees, living expenses, books and supplies, and mandatory health insurance.

Top Transfer Schools

Valencia College has transfer agreements with an extensive list of colleges and universities around the U.S. Of most interest to international students is Valencia's partnership with educational institutions in the state of Florida. These include the 31 private schools in the Independent Colleges and Universities of Florida (ICUF). Also included in transfer agreements are transfer guarantees to one of 12 public universities in Florida, including priority access to the University of Central Florida in Orlando.

Housing/Cost of Living

The monthly cost of a one-bedroom apartment in Orlando is $ 1,172.53 in the city center and $ 859.62 outside the city center. The cost of living index excluding rents is 74.59. For more information, go to Numbeo.com.

About the Location

Orlando, Florida is located in central Florida midway between cities on the Gulf of Mexico and Atlantic Ocean coasts. This area of Florida has flat topography, very green, with plenty of watery swamps and lakes. The Orlando metropolitan area has a population of more than two million people. The city and surrounding area became a center of citrus fruit production in the late 19th century, and in the early 20th century, Orlando began developing as a resort and conference center.

Tourism became even more important in 1971 when Walt Disney opened Walt Disney World. Other theme parks followed and now Orlando is known as the Theme Park Capital of the World. In addition to Disney World, tourists can visit Universal Orlando (Universal Studios), SeaWorld, and Gatorland, among others. These attractions bring in 62 million visitors each year.

Orlando is a high-tech and industrial center. There are also several movie studios in the area in and around Orlando. Film, theater, and music are important cultural aspects of Orlando. The city is also the home of two professional sports teams: Orlando Magic (basketball) and Orlando City SC (soccer). The city is home to several public and private colleges and universities, chief among them the University of Central Florida.

Orlando has a large Puerto Rican population as well as individuals from Caribbean countries such as Haiti and Jamaica.

The city has a humid, subtropical climate with warm, sunny winters, and hot, rainy summers. Florida is subject to hurricanes on both the east and west coasts, but hurricanes typically have less of an impact on Orlando because it is inland.

Find more information about Orlando at http://www.cityoforlando.net/ and http://www.visitorlando.com/

Name of College: **Washtenaw Community College**
Location: Ann Arbor, Michigan
College Website URL: http://www.wccnet.edu/
International Student Page:
http://www.wccnet.edu/services/internationalstudents/

Introduction

Washtenaw Community College is a public educational institution with about 13,000 students. The college follows a trimester system and offers an open admissions policy. There is no application fee. The student-to-faculty ratio is approximately 19 to 1. The college is located at one main campus in suburban Ann Arbor midway between downtown Ann Arbor and nearby Ypsilanti, Michigan.

The college had 81 students with F-1 visas in the winter of 2016, and additional international students with other visas. Countries sending the most international students to Washtenaw Community College are Korea, China, Vietnam, and Brazil. Most popular academic programs for international students are liberal arts, business, math and science/pre-engineering.

Academic Programs

Washtenaw Community College offers associate degrees and certificates in 18 different fields including business-related majors, communications, education, engineering, health, liberal arts, natural resources/conservation, and visual/performing arts. The college has three models for classes: the regular in-class learning with other students and a professor in the same classroom; online classes which take place entirely online, and blended classes which combine the in-class and online class model into a blended model. In addition, Washtenaw CC's English Department offers a full-range of English as a Second Language (ESL) courses for English-language learners.

Washtenaw Community College, Ann Arbor, Michigan

Services Offered

Washtenaw Community College has an International Student Center (ISC) located in the Student Union Building. According to the college website, "The ISC provides international orientation, ESL course advising, academic and vocational counseling, cultural adjustment counseling, student involvement and activities, and community resources."

Learning Support Services at Washtenaw CC includes individual and group tutoring options, services for disabled students, academic advising, and computer labs. The college offers the Computer-Adaptive Placement Assessment and Support System (COMPASS) tests to determine the correct class placement for students, and to ensure the greatest possibility of success. The COMPASS test has three components: reading, writing, and math. There is also a special COMPASS assessment test for ESL (English as a Second Language) students.

Test Scores

International students are required to offer proof of English-language proficiency. Minimum scores for TOEFL are 61 internet, and 500 paper test; for IELTS, 5.5; and for the MELAB (Michigan English Language Assessment Battery), a minimum score of 72 is required.

Tuition/Costs

Regular class tuition rates for international students are $246 for one credit hour and $738 for a three-credit class. The international students' tuition rate for distance learning/on-line classes is $112 for a one-credit class and $336 for a three-credit class. Additional fees apply as well.

Top Transfer Schools

Washtenaw Community College has articulation agreements with a long list of private and public colleges and universities. Perhaps most helpful to students intending to enter a four-year

Michigan university is the Michigan Transfer Agreement (MTA). According to college representatives, the MTA "allows for students to take elective courses at WCC which can be transferred to any of the public universities. The courses will differ depending on which institution they intend to study at after WCC, but allows students flexibility in taking courses before fully knowing where they would like to transfer and what they would prefer to study." Top transfer schools for Washtenaw CC students are: the University of Michigan Ann Arbor, Eastern Michigan University, and Michigan State University. The college provides Transfer Guides to a number of Michigan universities to help students in the transfer process.

Housing/Cost of Living

Washtenaw Community College provides housing for students as well as offering an Off-Campus Housing Service to help students find an apartment. The cost of a one-bedroom apartment in the city center is $ 1,277.27 and for a one-bedroom apartment away from the city center, $ 856.25. The cost-of-living index for Ann Arbor excluding rents is 68.53. For more specifics, go to Numbeo.com.

About the Location

Ann Arbor, home of Washtenaw Community College, is located in southeastern Michigan, a state in the northern middle of the United States near the Great Lakes. The metropolitan Ann Arbor area has a population of nearly 350,000. The nearest large city is Detroit. Ann Arbor is surrounded by an agricultural and fruit-growing area. Ann Arbor is a hilly city on the Huron River. The city is often called "Tree Town" because of its heavy forestation in residential areas and parks.

Ann Arbor's economy is strongly linked to the University of Michigan which employs thousands of local residents. There are several high-tech industries located in the city as well. The city has numerous cultural institutions and events, many linked to the

University of Michigan. These include museums, a Shakespeare festival, theater, symphony and ballet and annual art events.

Ann Arbor's climate is referred to as "humid continental." The Great Lakes have a strong influence on the climate. There are four distinct seasons. Winters are cold and snowy; summer is humid and warm; and spring and fall usually are mild but brief.

Learn more about Ann Arbor here: http://www.a2gov.org/Pages/default.aspx and here: https://www.visitannarbor.org/

Chapter 10. Students Speak

Danish Ali

Danish Ali is a mathematics student from Pakistan studying at Austin Community College in Austin, Texas. Saving money was a prime consideration when choosing a community college. Danish says, "I decided to study at a community college because international fees at a university level are way too much higher than community college. It's four times more. That's how I could save some money. Yes, I would recommend for people to study at a community college. You can save a lot on tuition fees by doing core courses here in lower costs."

What does he think is best and worst about living in the United States? "Best is- equality everywhere, no racism. Friendly atmosphere. Good law. Worst is it's a bit more expensive. International students are not allowed to work more than 20 hours at campus, and not even work off campus. It is hard to meet our own expenses most of the time. Fewer scholarships for international students."

What is Danish Ali's advice for students considering community college in the U.S.? "It's a very good option to consider an American community college. Be sure to research about your majors, and the field, and the living area and the state, etc."

Akram Alifliow

Akram Alfliow, a chemistry student from Saudi Arabia studying at Austin Community College, tells us how he came to study at an American community college. "I work for an oil company as a lab tech and I got a scholarship. However, the scholarship is only for associated degree. Therefore, I must go to a community college. ACC was one of the recommended colleges by my employer.

Austin Community College turned out to be a good choice for Akram. "Even if I were looking for a bachelor degree, I'd start studying at a community college. Small classes are better, and teachers in most cases are more helpful. So it's good to start at college to know the system of higher education, and figure out the best strategies for studying"

Akram considers the high cost of living to be the only problem he has encountered living in the United States.

He has three key areas of advice for international students thinking of studying in the U.S.

1. "Consider the high cost of living if he/she doesn't have a supporter."

2. "Before registering for classes, plan carefully, especially when you are going to take unfamiliar courses. For example, history of US or other cultures and governments courses, these courses require good reading and writing skills. Moreover, they contain a lot of new information that are not interesting usually since they don't apply or not important for international students. "

3. "It's better to study English at home country, and once you reach an acceptable level (around 5.5 in EILTS, e.g.), come to the U.S. to practice and develop your language skills. Never come with zero level."

Aldin Fafulovic

Aldin Fafulovic is a studying International and Global Studies at Wastenaw Community College in Ann Arbor, Michigan. He is from Bosnia and Herzegovina.

Aldin says, "I definitely recommend studying at a community college. Most community colleges have a wide range of diversity - students who are just like you from another country trying to reach their goals. This means that you can connect with them easily. Another reason why is the tuition itself. You get the same kind of quality education as if you'd go to a four-year university. Most of the instructors/professors are working part time at a community college and they teach at four-year universities as well. There are free resources to study well, and the support system is fascinating at community colleges. The whole experience makes studying fun, and it is a great choice/ investment for the future."

Regarding life in the U.S., Aldin says, "Living in the U.S. broadened my knowledge about opportunities and possibilities that were not even on my mind before I came here. With enough effort, I realized that I can choose what I want to do with my life, which is quite the opposite of what I've been experiencing back home where I had no options whatsoever, no matter how hard I tried. Also, having close friends as a support, people who love me and care about me. The worst aspects about living here are the adjustment to a different culture (culture shock), pace of life, and being away from family. Something that's difficult as well is understanding the process of taxes, documentation, understanding future possibilities like OPT and other options after graduation."

Aldin's advice for international students: "Be active in the college you'll be going to. Having good connections is important in this country. Be open to learn what is good about the American culture without losing the love for your own culture. Accept challenges, and pursue kindness, and you'll reap the fruit of it afterwards. Remember that you came to study in the US to reach your goals, and not to waste time on distractions, and enjoy doing that. Please, use the free resources a college offers, they are helpful."

"Owen" Guangli He

Guangli He is a Chinese student who uses the English name "Owen." He has been studying petroleum engineering at Austin Community College, and he hopes to transfer to the University of Texas at Austin. He decided to go to community college for the same reasons as other students – lower cost and to improve his English.

"To be honest, my English reading section was pretty bad when I took my SAT and ACT. I didn't have a shot to get into UT Austin with my standard test score. But now, with my GPA in community college, I have a pretty good chance of getting in. Also, community colleges are cheaper. The tuition here is a third of what UT charges.

"Austin Community College is definitely an amazing place. The professors here are very helpful. There all free tutoring in the learning lab throughout the week. Also the facilities are advanced as well!"

Regarding his experience living in the United States, "Best, everything is generally easier and more relaxed. I get to do what I'm interested in and also moving toward my career dream and goals. Worst, people are generally less connected. People are nicer but it is hard to build deep connection and relationship. I think it has something to do with that many people who are in community college have a lot more things going on in their life. I know a lot of them have a full time job other than school."

Owen's advice for international students studying in the U.S.: "Manage your time well can get you a good score easily and have a lot more fun other than school. And also have more friends can make your life happier and easier too!"

Marcela Gutierrez Castillo

Marcela Gutierrez is from Nuevo León, Mexico. She has been studying business administration at Pima Community College in Tucson, Arizona.

She tells us: "Yes, I really recommend study in a community college. I think community colleges prepare you really good for any degree you're taking. Some of them are better in some majors, but I think all of them will prepare you to get a degree. Also for people who want to transfer to a four year university, a community college is a great place to start. It's a cheaper option and it can help you save some money."

Regarding life in the U.S., Marcela says, "The best aspects living in the United States are that I'm having a really good education, I've learn a lot of different cultures, I've been improving my English, and I've learned a lot of new things in this country. The only worst aspect is that I'm away from home and my family."

Her advice: "For international students study in America it's really expensive, even if you are at a community college. So my advice is to make sure you have an scholarship before you get to school in America."

Miguel Hernandez

Mexican student Miguel Hernandez studies music business performance and technology. He chose Austin Community College "because it is less expensive, and because it was easier to begin to get to know the system, and deal with language gap. I recommend [a community college] because it is cheaper. You can experiment with your major, and change your mind without wasting as much.

The school seems to give you more attention than in a university. However the student, and general atmosphere is not good. For Miguel, the best part of his experience living in the U.S. is "the opportunities, the knowledge, the city, the relation with different cultures." The worst part includes "the cultural change, the different rules, the limitations in communication due to language."

His advice for international students: "Learn how the system works. Learn not to be ethnocentric. Do not be afraid to ask questions. Learn who can give good answers. Stay out of your comfort zone."

Petra Jansen-Kuite

Petra Jansen-Kuite is from the Netherlands. She is studying philosophy at Austin Community College. She explains that her experience is a little different than many international students. Her sense of humor and enthusiastic spirit come through in her words.

"I graduated high school in 1997. I figured it would be smarter for me to start with studying at a community college and not throw myself into the deep end right away. Eventually my plan changed and I decided I wanted to stay in the States, so before graduating I changed my major to a few others: nursing, pharmacy tech, and surgery tech. This would give me a better chance of obtaining a green card and paying for a four-year university. The difference in tuition would have been well worth the trouble of staying in a community college first. This plan failed, however, as I had to leave the States to resolve some issues back home.

"I do recommend studying at a community college. As far as I know the tuition is lower and when you don't plan on changing your major it is not too hard to enroll in a 4-year university afterwards. The best part about studying in the States was the dramatic improvement of my language skills. English had always been easy for me, but now it's become the language I use most of the time, even here in the Netherlands. Having learned so much about the English language, not even having studied English in particular, I learned (and still do) a lot about the origin and original meaning of words and sayings. This, in turn, teaches me about different cultures and habits, among many other things.

"I also enjoyed learning so many different things about the people of the United States. Us Europeans tend to have a somewhat negative view of Americans, and of course we all know the U.S. is a huge country. However, we never quite grasp the fact that there are many different types Americans. We expect Americans to understand that Europe is made up of a lot of countries but we don't realize that 'America' is pretty much the same thing as the European Union. People from Texas are not the same as people from New York, or even Louisiana or Kansas. And that is only because of the fact that all Americans speak 'American', have one flag and call that chunk of land 'a country', which is run by one President. We simply forget that even in such a tiny place as the Netherlands there are two official languages, 12 provinces, and at least as many cultures and dialects. So why would the U.S.A. be any different?

"Another very good aspect was finding that there is nothing wrong with the level of education in the States. We Dutch just don't know how to teach, our teachers suffer from burn-out, because they just don't know how to make their classes interesting and entertaining. It seems they lack enthusiasm and have too much to teach in way too little time, because of all the bureaucratic nonsense and the *neck breathing* government.

"The worst part was realizing I had to take U.S. Government and Politics and Texas Government and Politics. I knew this was the moment something interesting was going to happen because I, like so many Europeans, figured I knew what was wrong with the States. During the first class I found myself wondering how on earth I could have been so horribly wrong. That was the changing point. Combine this with U.S. History I and II and 'enter the somewhat-enlightened Petra.' I could never have done a better job at starting and building a new country. I had been much too arrogant ('oh my, what is it that so many of us accuse so many of you of again.....?') It basically comes down to the fact that the worst and best have the same origin and the worst actually caused the best. And the love I have for your country now is immense. Your beautiful country gave me peace, happiness, love. Thank you!"

Petra's advice for international students: "Keep an open mind, and remember, you are there to learn, not to teach. There is a time for that when you return to your home country."

Ileana N. Kraus

Ileana N. Kraus is a German student who is studying musical performance at Austin Community College. She chose to study at a community college because, "I didn't know yet which college I wanted to get my bachelor's at, and I wasn't sure if I wanted to pursue a bachelor degree at all. Community college gave me the opportunity to start on my studies. I do recommend [community college], especially if you come from another country and don't have a very specific plan. It gives the opportunity to understand the college system in the U.S. better. If you know what exactly you want, I wouldn't recommend it, and instead pursue your choice of college. It is good though if you need more time, but don't want to wait to start."

Regarding living in the U.S., Ileana says, "I am free to pursue my dream of playing music. The music scene in the U.S. gives more opportunities than in my home country, especially with the music I play. I play fiddle (violin) and I sing. I play a lot of different styles. Jazz is definitely one of them. I also love to play Bluegrass music, Blues, and all kinds of other styles. I just got back from a fiddle workshop here in Texas. I absolutely loved it. My sister and I have a band together, and our songs are a mix of pop, Mediterranean, jazz and folk music."

Ileana's advice for international students: "Always ask an advisor who knows about rules for international students. Be careful, though, a lot of advisors give wrong or incomplete information due to the complexity of different cases. Double check, read, and communicate with other international students, advisors, teachers and if really necessary talk to a lawyer. And never give up. There's always a way!"

Gabriela da Rosa Masiero

Gabriela da Rosa Masiero is from Brazil. She is majoring in journalism and has a theater minor at Valencia College. A fellow-Brazilian friend, Luciana Giron, introduced Gabriela to Valencia College. Gabriela explains, "She introduced me to Valencia, where I studied English for almost four months and then I went to the "other side" (college, this is how they called it). I decided to stay because of the price comparing with the big universities, but mainly because I feel like home in Valencia. They helped you to know all these new information and life, and you have the opportunity to take baby steps first. I'm not in a rush at all! "

Does she recommend community college? "For sure. Valencia has amazing resources, things that I can't believe until today, and I'm still impressed. We have all the support that we need in there like the Math center, which you have professors available for you and amazing resource such as the Writing and Speech center, where you can sit with someone who will help you with your work for classes, languages center, amazing libraries, etc. Valencia still surprising me after two semesters!"

Worst and best aspects of life in the United States: "The best is the quality of life. The safety, the structure, everything around me. I feel good and alive living here, and feel that I have value for who I am. The culture of respect is amazing, I've been learning so much with Americans, including the habit of doing this right to receive it right. The worst part is the distance and some aspects that I miss from my culture. I miss my family so much, and sometimes I still can't believe that they are so far from me. I caught myself many times wondering if I was losing something being here (my brother growing, for example). When it comes to the culture, I miss some Brazilians habits, like being with my friends all the time, mainly about my social life. I'm working on that and started to hang out with Brazilians here too! My academic life is my priority right now; I'm focused on leave a legacy, being known for my determination and capacity."

Gabriela's advice: "Come. Don't think twice. Valencia will bring you a new vision of the world. Be open to the cultures, since Valencia is an amazing place which receives people from around the world. Enjoy learning more about that as well! We have advisors available all the time. Go talk to them every week about your classes and doubts. Talk to your professor, show them that you are interested. This makes ALL the difference. They are amazing and will help you a lot! Get involved with the activities and events, it's an amazing opportunity to get to know people and feel like Valencia is your home. Participate, be there, and use all the resources you can. Here, you won't be successful only if you don't want to!"

Aya Nagata

Aya Nagata is a Japanese student studying business at Cabrillo College in California. Aya recommends study at a community college because, "it is much cheaper, and still it is possible to get high [level] of education. Also, the opportunity of seeing cool people is same even at community college."

Of her experience living in the U.S., she says, "The best aspect living in U.S. is learning different ways of thinking and seeing many people with gaining new acknowledgement. The bad aspect is that I am not citizen of America, so there are many struggles in my life such as needing a Social Security number for getting a job." She advises international students to "stay positive and seize the opportunity of making friends. It is all about people who surround you."

Catherine Pérez

Catherine Pérez is from Venezuela. She is studying digital media at Valencia College in Orlando, Florida. Catherine tells us: "I already have a Bachelor's Degree in Mass Communications which I earned almost 5 years ago at Universidad Católica Andrés Bello (UCAB) in my country, Venezuela. When I finished my studies around 2012, I knew I wanted to keep learning and "keep my teeth sharp" in the communications area so I went in 2013 to Orlando to improve my English. I fell in love with Florida, even though it was not the first time I went. After that I decided that I wanted to get more knowledge in my professional area in the U.S.

During a couple of years I was looking for a Master's Degree. Unfortunately, it was too expensive for my family and I, so I started looking for certifications. Then I found this program at Valencia College which I knew since I saw it that it was just perfect for me......About year and a half ago I found this degree in Digital Media which complement the Digital Production area, and also the track in Journalism as I always wanted. So, like I said, it is just perfect! And also cheaper.

Her thoughts on studying at an American community college: "Yes, I highly recommend it. I believe that people need to work for what they want always considering their options. I have noticed living here in the U.S that many American families really deal with the hard decision of sending their kids to college/university or being drowning in debts. This has captured my attention, because international students pay twice and sometimes more than an American resident, but I can tell many people in the U.S struggle with this.

"Therefore, for those who are worried about the money, community college is an excellent option, either if they want to get their whole degree or just starting the first 2 years of the career which is a very smart option if you ask me. Like I said before, small steps are still steps! This is my second semester at Valencia, and my first community college experience, and I believe it definitely will bring more pros than cons. To me being successful depends more in working hard and taking advantage of the opportunities that a place like this can offer. It is cheaper and despite what many people say or stereotype, the quality of education can be really high. I think I can say this having experience studying in both, university and now community college. Plus, it is also beneficial for those that are not quite sure what path they want to take. I remember being at my university in Caracas, and I used to see a bunch of confused students who did not have idea about what they really want to do, so they were changing careers all the time."

Regarding living in the U.S., Catherine says: "Let´s start with the worst. I would say that what has been more difficult to me is to be away from home, my family and my dog! No kidding! ....For the best aspects, well where can I start? I do love and admire this country since I was a kid. To me the culture is amazing. I have noticed that America is the middle point for many people. For example, for those who come from Latin America, we are looking for progress and order. On the other hand, for many people coming from Europe, for example, they come to America looking for more freedom maybe. I say this because talking to some friends I can tell that in their countries they don´t feel "free" enough. It is funny how things work out. Different points of view and goals have USA as a common place to meet. Another aspect of Americans I DO admire is the passion and love they have for their land. I think it is admirable how proud they all, and I mean ALL are of their country. This is definitely the key for the progress of this country, one of the best in the world, if not the best one!

"Finally, wherever you go, with a degree or work experience from a country like this is always a plus, and just the experience of being here, experience the life style, its people. I particularly feel blessed, and it is an experience I highly recommend. You learn way more than just academic knowledge."

Catherine's advice: "I would say DO IT! It is a great experience. It will not only open your eyes and mind, but also a whole new world of possibilities for your future. I would also recommend showing interest while they are studying. I have noticed that professors in America are very helpful if you show you are interested in learning and improving. Do not feel afraid! Ask, make appointments with them, and show your best.

"Last but not least. Yes, you will feel homesick and scared, but it is nothing to be worried about. There are 3 stages in this process of being an international student:

1- You feel super excited before arriving.

2-Homesick mode on! You will have second thought, but trust me, give it a few weeks.

3-Adaptation. Once you create your routine, start talking to people, making simple little things like going to Publix or Starbucks or any other place, things will fall into place. You will be building a new beautiful life."

Stephanie Gorentzvaig Rocco

Stephanie Rocco is from Brazil and majoring in biomedicine at Valencia College in Orlando, Florida. She plans to continue her medical studies. Stephanie lists her reasons for choosing a community college:

"There are a few reasons why I decided to first attend a community college:

- Community colleges tend to have smaller classes (at least Valencia College is limited to 30 people per class) and since English is my second language I feel more comfortable being in an environment where I do not have to be ashamed of my accent by asking a question in front of a few people rather than 150 people or more.
- Professors are very open office and helpful. In fact it is easier to have a one-on-one moment with your professor in case you have concerns in regards the material or even the class.
- It is cheaper, especially when you are an international student and pay out-of-state tuition.

- International offices at a community colleges tend to be more supportive and helpful with their students since there is a limited amount of foreign students.

"I do recommend anyone to begin first at a community college. A university can cause a huge impact on you if you are coming from a high school setting or even if you are coming from another country. It is good to first settle and get used to a college education in a place here you will find more academic counseling, advising support, and smaller classes."

Regarding life in the United States: "Being far away from your family is not easy, but once you get used to it and adapt to the system, things tend to get easier and smoother. I think the worst aspect was being far from my family. The best I would say the life and how the system here works better. I come from a third world country where there is inflation and violence. In the U.S. we can feel that we are in a first world country, where the economy works and protection exists. I also this that people are more respectful in this country, they respect your space and tend to be more polite."

Her advice for international students: "One can get a lot of support and help at a community college. Do not hesitate to ask for help, even if you have any personal issue. I have learned a great deal at my community college, and I also found a second family at Valencia. I made good friends, people from around the world as well. Get involved with clubs and organizations on campus. These also add a lot to your leadership, self-growth, social relations, and also there's community service which I appreciate the most."

Ty Tejada

Ty Tejeda is a student from the Dominican Republic who is currently studying business administration at Washtenaw Community College in Michigan.

"I highly recommend studying at a community college such as my current college WCC (Washtenaw Community College). Community colleges are affordable and they offer the necessary tools for students to easily learn and be successful to achieve their goals. I've found the staff and professors that work at this wonderful school are not only qualified professionals in their areas of expertise, but are genuinely interested in the success of their students."

Regarding the best and worst parts of living in the U.S., Ty says: "My experience in being in America and learning about the diverse cultures, trying new foods and experiencing different life styles has been one of the best things that's ever happened to me. I enjoy the change of seasons I experience here in America and activities such as snowboarding, waterskiing, and many outdoor activities that I was unable to do back in the Dominican Republic. At the same time some of the cultural differences have been very difficult for me to adapt to. I came from a country where people are more friendly and willing to open their hearts to others, so when I got here it was really difficult for me to understand why some people were indifferent to my friendly approaches. Nowadays I know how to deal with this situation."

Ty's advice for international students: "Don't be afraid of the unknown. It's worth a try, it's worth to fight for, and it's worth to make a sacrifice. Be hungry for knowledge, be willing to learn from others, and be willing to accept others and their ways. Always be polite and respectfully, be a person of good values and most of all, be a good ambassador from your country."

Thang Khan Sian Khai

Thang Khan Sian Khai is majoring in digital media production at the Isaacson School for New Media at Colorado Mountain College. He is from Myanmar/Burma.

He tells us: "Coming from a medium income family, going to community college is one of the best choices that we have. Moreover, when you don't know what you want to be, exploring in community college has more advantage than four-year colleges or universities. I definitely recommend students to start at the

169

community college unless they know what they want exactly. Otherwise, I believe it is going to be a waste of time and money when you realized you don't want to follow that path in four year college."

Regarding life in the United States, he says: "Best is especially Colorado Mountain College. They take you as a family and you can get one-to-one relationship with the teachers but also counselors and faculty members. The worst is that sometime you may miss food, someone who can speak the same language with you, and you face cultural differences."

His advice for international students: "Prepare to be changed and accept the challenges. Otherwise, you may not able to enjoy." And last not least, "Ask".

Ederson Lugubone Tobisawa

Ederson Tobisawa is a Brazilian student majoring in biochemistry at Washtenaw Community College in Ann Arbor. He plans to study medicine in the U.S.

Ederson tells us: "I definitely recommend international students to start up college at a community college. Personally, I have grown a lot since my first year of college, including my English skills. I believe that community colleges can provide a less intimidating environment compared to an university. Also, at community colleges you have the option to build up a closer relationship with professors and staff, which I believe it is essential when we are far from home.

"The worst aspect for me about living in the U.S is the long distance from my family. At the beginning it was extremely tough to deal with the fact that I was 5000 miles away from them I would have to live by myself.

"Finally, my advice for other international students is to GO FOR IT. Even though my challenges have come along with my decision to living abroad, we definitely learn a lot of ourselves and everything that we are capable of. I would never exchange my experience here in the U.S with anything else."

Erlie Ulysse

Erlie Ulysee is a student from Haiti who is studying business administration and management at Valencia College in Florida. Lower costs were a big part of Erlie's decision to study first at a community college. She explains: "Since international students pay out of pocket and since the price per credit hour for an international student is three to four times more expensive than resident student, economically, it is best to start at a community college instead of a four year college or university. Because it not only it is cheaper, but most of the times, we international students are required to take some English preparation classes that most universities do not really have available at any time during the academic year unlike community colleges."

Erlie continues: "I highly recommend any student to start with a community college, not just because of pricing but also because they have smaller classroom and they are easier to adapt to.....The best aspect of living in the United States is the brand new "experience" living in the united states, learning and getting use to another system than the one that you were raised on. The worst aspect would be being coping with being away from friends and family. To me, the best way to cope, it's to get more involved, keep yourself busy. For example, participate in study groups, clubs (some colleges has some cultural clubs), volunteer and get involved within the community and school. That way you get to meet new people and sometimes people from your own culture.

"My advice for students considering to study at an American community college would be to know their options and carefully consider everything when it comes to being an international student."

Jaime Sklavos Walsh

Jaime Walsh recently earned an Associate of Arts degree with an emphasis in Theater from Colorado Mountain College. Jaime is from Canada. She decided to enroll at a community college because, "I didn't know what I wanted to do. To have the option of going to a two-year school, and getting all of the required classes out of the way seem like the right decision. I also love theatre. I studied it in high school, and knew I wanted to continue that education, but didn't know where I wanted to study it."

Can Jaime recommend a community college? "Yes! To go from a high school setting with 25 kids in a class room, to a university with 300 people in a lecture hall is terrifying! I was able to have a small class room size, know every student by name and was able to have one-on-one interactions with my teachers, and even now I am able to e-mail or call them for advice."

Regarding the worst aspects of living in the U.S., Jaime makes several good points. "In so many ways Canada and the States are very similar, and yes, we pronounce things funny once in a while, and our money is different. But what I have really noticed (at least where I went to school) there isn't a lot of diversity. I grew up in Toronto, one of the biggest melting pots in the world where I could experience any culture I wanted by traveling just a few short miles. I am part Greek, and have olive skin, and people assume I speak Spanish. It makes me sad that people can't distinguish the difference between cultures. I also miss free health care. Did it suck paying 13% tax in Toronto? Yes, but I would rather pay the tax then be terrified walking into a doctor's office or a hospital worried about how much it may cost me. This goes without saying, but I also miss Tim Horton's (a Canadian fast-food restaurant chain). They really need a good doughnut place down here!"

Regarding the best aspects, Jaime says, "Why is everyone so friendly down here?! I though Canadians were supposed to be the nice ones! If ever I was lost or need help I felt like anyone would be willing to point me in the right direction. I met my husband at Colorado Mountain College. He is the nicest, most good hearted, caring person I have ever known. Everything is a lot cheaper than it is in Canada. I love that I can afford everything, and still have some money left over (also to have Amazon everything so quickly down here is amazing!). There is no traffic! Even when I visit Denver it isn't as bad as Toronto! There wasn't any academic competition. I grew up in an Asian part of the city, and we were judged very harshly on what was good and bad in school. I believe that's why I succeed in the States because I didn't feel critiqued. I was enjoying my education."

Her advice for international students thinking of studying at an American community college: "Explore the whole country, not just the state you choose to study in. Every state has something beautiful, and fantastic to share. Road trips are so much fun especially when you have time to kill. I had a few friends that couldn't go home for Thanksgiving weekend, so we drove to Utah and had a blast!"

Eri Watanabe

Eri Watanabe is a Japanese student studying speech communication at Austin Community College.

Here are Eri's reasons for choosing a community college. "I decided to go a community college first rather than going four year university for several reasons. First, the tuition is much lower for community colleges than four year universities. Second, it was easier for me to get into a community colleges because the English skill requirement is not as high as four-year institutions, which enables me to develop my English skills by taking some college level classes. Third, the classes are relatively easier at community colleges, which helps me to earn good grades and gives me an opportunity to transfer into a better four-year universities that I was not able to get in at first. I would recommend studying at a community college for those benefits I mentioned above. However, I don't recommend a community college for those students who already have enough English skills to go to a four-year university because the universities relatively have better educations, bachelors-level classes and even scholarships."

Eri's thoughts on living in the United States: "The best aspects are that it is possible to learn variety of cultures from all over the world (at least by living in Austin, I think so). The worst aspects are that it is illegal for international students with F-1 visa to work out side of the campus or they will be deported. This restriction has been bringing financial problem to some international students who want to study in the United States."

Any advice for international students considering an American community college? "For such students, I will strongly recommend to have enough financial support and English skills for their academic success in the United States. In addition, if it's possible, they had better have certain level of connection with people who live in both the U.S. and the students' home country so that the students can ask them help just in case."

"Harry" Xinran Yang

Xinran Yang is a student from Guilin, China who earned his associate degree in liberal arts. He is currently studying computer science at Austin Community College. He uses the English name "Harry."

He chose community college over a four-year college because "I couldn't get into one because my English was not good enough. ACC had fairly simple admission process, and the application process at universities intimidated me. Also a community college is more affordable.

"I think a four-year college has more resources for a student/international student to be successful. If the international student came to the U.S. at a young age, it is easier for him/her to make friends, get to know the culture when studying in an environment with people around the same age. Studying in a community college also requires the student to have more self-

discipline to succeed. I'd say a four-year college/university is the
better choice if the student has the financial resources.

"The best aspect [about living in the U.S.] is that comparing to
the environment in China, people here are generally more tolerant
and less judgmental toward people with different ideas, social and
economic backgrounds. There's also less competition. The worst
aspect is that my future is uncertain in this county as long as I am a
foreigner. It gives me pressure every time I think about it. Dealing
with this pressure constantly becomes a part of my life in the US. "

Harry's advice for international students: "First of all, if
money is not an issue, study hard and try to go to a university
directly. If not, then utilize every resource possible to try to get an
associate degree quickly and transfer to a university. If the student's
goal is to survive in the U.S., or to finish the education and go back
to the home country, a bachelor's degree is the minimum
requirement. Community college is really good for Americans that
look for continuing education, but it should only be a stepping
stone for international students.

Chapter 11. Glossary of Terms

academic advising: College staff help students to understand academic requirements and to choose coursework that will lead to a degree or certificate

academic credit: course work, tests, or other activity that is applied toward requirements resulting in a degree

academic program: courses and other requirements that will result in a degree upon completion

accreditation: The U.S. has several regional educational accrediting agencies responsible for reviewing college academic programs and determining if the college meets academic standards. Examples of accrediting agencies are: New England Association of Schools and Colleges, Higher Learning Commission, and Northwest Accreditation Commission.

add a class: For a short period (usually one week or 10 days) following college-wide registration for classes, students are allowed to register for an additional class or classes. Students can also withdraw from a class during this period, often called "dropping a class."

Advanced Placement (AP) exams: Colleges and universities often grant academic credit in a specific subject area if a student passes an Advanced Placement (AP) test in that subject area. AP exams are available in a number of subjects, including English and other languages, biology, chemistry, mathematics, physics, psychology, history, and more. Students typically take the AP exams during their final year of high school.

American Dream: The idea that every American citizen, regardless of race, ethnicity, gender, or origin, will have an opportunity to achieve the dream of prosperity, success, and a happy life by working hard and showing personal responsibility and initiative.

articulation agreement: A formal agreement between two educational institutions that allows credits earned at one institution to transfer to the other. Typically this means that credits earned at a community college will transfer to a 4-year college or university and count toward a bachelor's degree. *See also* transfer partnerships

assessment tests: Tests given to all college students, not just international students, to assess student academic proficiency and to place students in the appropriate class.

associate degree: A college degree earned after two years of academic study at a community college. The degree program typically includes some required courses and some elective courses.

ATM (automatic teller machine): Most banks in the U.S. provide their customers with ATM machines to engage in basic transactions such as deposits and withdrawals. ATM machines are available in various locations such as grocery stores and in shopping malls. The bank customer uses a bank-issued credit card to access ATM services. You must enter a PIN number (personal identification number) to use the ATM card.

auto insurance: There are levels of auto insurance coverage. The basic coverage is "liability insurance" which will pay for any injuries to another person and damages to that person's property that you cause in a motor vehicle accident. Liability insurance is legally required of all car owners. Owners can also purchase auto insurance that will cover theft and general damage to the car as well as liability expenses.

bank balance: the amount of money in your bank account

big box stores: large, warehouse-like stores that carry a wide range of items such as food, clothing, toys, auto supplies, garden supplies, etc.

bills (currency): refers to paper money: twenty-dollar bill, five-dollar bill, etc.

bills (statement of charges): an amount of money you owe that is written in a statement, typically with a due date
brush-up workshops: extra classes or workshops to review information and academic content that you already know in order to prepare you for assessment tests

cash (currency): refers to money in the form of paper bills or coins
CBT: computer-based test
certificate: a document that is earned by taking specialized academic courses in a specific area.
certificate of eligibility: *See* **I-20 form (certificate of eligibility)**
checking and **saving accounts**: Typically checking accounts are used to pay bills and receive deposits of money. Savings accounts are used to save money. Savings accounts often receive interest payments from the bank for the amount in the account.
civil liberties: individual rights protected by law such as freedom of speech, freedom of religion, and the right to a fair trial
closed class: a class with a pre-determined number of allowed students that is now full
College Level Examination Program (CLEP): CLEP tests are standardized tests that assess your knowledge of college-level subject areas. If you pass the tests, you may be able to earn college credits without taking the college course. CLEP tests are created and administered by the College Board.
community college: a two-year institution of higher learning that can grant an associate degree and/or professional certificates
conditional admission: A student is admitted to the college, but the student must finish specific courses or meet an academic standard such as a specified-level of English-language proficiency.
continuing education units (CEU): additional post-graduate courses to keep individuals up-to-date in their chosen field
convenience store: small stores with a limited number of items for sale, but open for longer hours than typical stores

cosigner: a person who signs an agreement to borrow money with another person such as an international student.

cost of living: costs of daily life including rent, food, telephone, transportation, etc.

counseling: Counseling is a consultation with a professional in a specific area such as financial counseling, academic counseling, or personal counseling to help you deal with personal problems.

Craig'sList: An online market in major cities where you can look for items to buy, items to sell, job listings, and more. *See* https://www.craigslist.org/about/sites#US

credit cards: plastic cards you use at a store to pay for items you want to buy. The credit card company will send you a monthly statement of what you purchased, and how much you owe. Essentially, a credit card is a way of borrowing money temporarily to make a purchase.

credit union: a financial institution owned by its members

Curricular Practical Training (CTP): jobs integrated into a specific academic class

daylight saving time: In the U.S., many states will twice yearly change the time by one hour.

debit card: a card used to automatically pay for items as in a grocery store. You must enter a PIN number to use the debit card. Money is immediately deducted from your account for the purchase.

deposit (rental): When renting an apartment, you will be required to pay an amount of money to cover damage you may have caused and any rent you failed to pay.

designated school official (DSO): an employee of your college who is appointed to assist F and M visa students

dormitory, dormitories, dorms: Some colleges, especially four-year colleges, provide housing for students on campus. Students share a room, and often eat in the dormitory cafeteria.

driver's license: a legal document allowing you to drive a motor vehicle. To acquire a driver's license, you must pass a written test and a driving test, and pay a fee.
DS-160: form to apply online for a nonimmigrant visa

early action: Indicates that you applied early and were accepted early. You do not have to accept immediately. Early action programs are not legally binding.
early decision: Indicates that you applied early and you were accepted early, and now you are legally required to enroll. Early decision programs are legally binding.
elective courses: courses that are not required to earn a degree, but that may add knowledge in your chosen subject area
Electronic System for Travel Authorization (ESTA): Individuals in the Visa Waiver Program must be registered with ESTA, and get approval to travel to the United States.
endorse a check: write your name on the back of a check
ESL: English as a Second Language
ethnic markets: stores that specialize in food and goods from a specific culture or country, e.g. Ethiopian food
extracurricular activities: Participation in non-academic programs such as sports, music or art, or community volunteer work.

fees. Money amounts charged to students in addition to tuition to cover educational costs such as science laboratories, library, or other services.
freshman: Students in their first year of college are called freshmen.
furnished apartment: an apartment that already has furniture when you rent it

garage sale/yard sale: a short-term sale of used items, often on a weekend, offered by an individual or family in their garage or yard
GED: General Education Diploma. This is equivalent to a high school diploma.

grade point average (GPA): Your scores from all the courses you've taken are averaged together to calculate your grade point average.

groceries: food, including produce and meats, as well as household items such as soap

hardware store: specialty stores that carry tools, wood, paint, plumbing supplies, gardening supplies, etc.

homestay: a housing arrangement in which a student lives with a family

I-20 form (certificate of eligibility): This form is issued by an educational institution to a student seeking an F1 visa to study in the U.S. The I-20 form certifies that you are eligible for an F1 visa.

ibT: internet-based test

IELTS: International English Language Testing System

in-state tuition and fees. *See* residency and resident fees

Intensive English Program (IEP): Students study in an intensive and concentrated program of English courses. IEP is not the same as English as a Second Language (ESL) classes taken along with other college courses.

junior: Students in their third year of college are called juniors.

landlord: person responsible for renting housing and solving issues such as plumbing problems

lease (rental): a legal agreement that details your obligation to the apartment owner, and the apartment owner/manager's obligation to you. Leases are often one year in length.

liability insurance: insurance on your motor vehicle that will pay for any injuries to another person and damages to that person's property that you caused in a motor vehicle accident. Liability insurance is legally required of all motor vehicle owners.

liberal arts: a general academic program designed to provide broad knowledge and skills. Liberal arts programs usually include a wide range of courses in sciences, humanities, and language and literature.

license plate (motor vehicle): metal identification plate with a unique number that is attached to the rear of the vehicle

major and **minor**: Courses chosen in a student's chosen field of study. For example, a student may have a major in business administration and a minor in accounting, or a major in biology and a minor in chemistry.

manager (apartment): person responsible for renting housing and solving issues such as plumbing problems

naturalized citizen: refers to individuals who immigrated to the U.S. and became U.S. citizens. Becoming a naturalized citizen involves meeting eligibility requirements, becoming a permanent legal residency, paying an application fee, passing civics and English tests, and attending a naturalization service.

nonresident fees: Many colleges and universities have residency requirements. Typically the student must have lived in the state for at least one year in order to qualify for lower residents' fees. International students are usually classified as nonresidents. These fees are also called **out-of-state fees.**

open class: a class with a pre-determined number of students allowed in the class, and that now has openings for additional students

Optional Practical Training (OPT): An international student can apply for and receive one year of paid employment in the student's field of study. Students do not have to change their visas to participate in OPT, but they must get authorization from their school advisors.

orientation: sessions that introduce the college and college procedures to new students

out-of-state tuition and fees. *See* nonresident fees

PayPal: an electronic commerce company that allows you to receive money and pay bills online using your credit card

PBT: paper-based test

PIN number (personal identification number): unique numbers used with debit cards and bank cards

pharmacy: A store where prescription drugs ordered by a doctor and non-prescription drugs are sold, usually under the direction of a professional pharmacist.

placement tests:. Tests given to all college students, not just international students, to assess student proficiency, and to place students in the appropriate class.

plagiarism: taking another's work and claiming it is your own work. This usually refers to passages in a book or other text..

prerequisite course: a course or program that must be completed before registering for a another more advance course or program. Example: algebra is a prerequisite course before taking calculus

produce: fresh fruits and vegetables

registration (class): the process of selecting and signing up for an academic course

registration (vehicle): a legal document verifying that your motor vehicle is registered with the state where you live, and that it has been inspected and is in good working order. Usually states require a yearly renewal of the registration.

required courses: college courses that are required to earn a degree.

residency and **resident fees**: A resident is a person who has lived in a state for a certain period of time, often one year. Students who are residents typically pay lower tuition than students who are not residents of a state.

rolling admissions: the college will accept your application for entry over an extended time period, for example, six months.

room and board: refers to the costs associated with renting a room or apartment and also receiving meals (board)

scam: a fraudulent scheme to steal your money

seniors: Students in their fourth year of college are called seniors.

SEVIS. *See* Student and Exchange Visitor Information System

SEVP certified: colleges and universities certified by the Student and Exchange Visitor Program (SEVP).

Social Security: A U.S. federal government insurance program for retired and disabled individuals. Workers pay taxes into the Social Security program during their work life, and then they receive a monthly stipend during their retirement years.

Social Security number: The U.S. federal government assigns a Social Security number to workers or the purpose of deducting social security tax from wages. International students who are employed must have a Social Security number.

STEM field: science, technology, engineering, mathematics

Student and Exchange Visitor Program (SEVP): program of the U.S. Immigration and Customs Enforcement (ICE) which is a part of the U.S. Department of Homeland Security. According to Homeland Security's website, "SEVP monitors F and M students and their dependents while in the United States to ensure that rules and regulations are followed by international students. The program also certifies schools to allow them to enroll F or M students. International students studying in the United States can only attend an SEVP-certified school.

sophomore: Students in their second year of college are called sophomores.

Student and Exchange Visitor Information System (SEVIS): an online system that maintains current information about international students and exchange visitors, as well as SEVP-certified schools and exchange-visitor programs.

supermarkets: large grocery stores with a wide range of food and household items for sale

technical college: a two-year college that prepares students for employment in a chosen field immediately after graduation

AMERICAN COMMUNITY COLLEGES

thrift store: stores where used items are sold, often as a fund-raiser for a charitable organization

title (vehicle): a legal document stating your ownership of a motor vehicle

time zones: The U.S. is divided into several zones with a one-hour time difference between each zone.

TOEFL: Test of English as a Foreign Language

transcripts: official record of courses you have completed and your scores

transfer partners and **transfer partnerships**: A community college participates in an agreement with a four-year university that allows a community-college graduate guaranteed acceptance into the partner university provided that the student has all the academic requirements. Under transfer agreements, community-college course credits will transfer to the partner four-year university. *See also* **articulation agreement**

traveler's checks: checks issues by your bank to use in other countries when traveling

2+2 degree programs: Earn an associate degree in your first two years, then transfer to a university and finish your bachelor's degree in two additional years.

undergraduate: four-year academic program leading to a bachelor's degree. Also refers to a person studying for a bachelor's degree.

unfurnished apartment: an apartment that has no furniture when you rent it

utilities or utility bills: costs associated with electricity, gas, and water, and often telephone service

wait list: If a class is full and there are no more seats in the class, you may enter your name on a wait list. If another student drops out of the class, you will take that student's place and enroll in the class.

yard sale/garage sale: a short-term sale, often on a weekend, offered by an individual or family in their garage or yard to sell used items

INDEX

academic advising, 81–84

accreditation, 23, 28–29, 45

admission, applying for, 24, 45–57

    documents and forms for, 50–52

    providing proof of funding, 48–50

    proving English proficiency, 52–54

Advanced Placement (AP) exams, 81

advising, academic, 81–84

Affidavit of Support (form I-134), 49, 76

American culture, 22, 94/-95, 115–17

American Dream, 114

American people, 108–14

American values, 113–14

Amtrak trains, 73

apartments, renting or leasing, 95–96

Arrival and Departure Record (form I-94), 69–70

articulation agreements, 21, 30. *See also* transfer partnerships

assessment tests, 53, 77–79

associate degree, 15

ATM machines, 90

Austin Community College, Texas, *16*, 17, 19, 40, 53, 77, 122–27

bachelor's degree, 18

bank accounts, 89–90

Bunker Hill Community College, Massachusetts, 17, 29, 32, 46, 78, 81, 127–31

business/economics/accounting studies, 40

Cabrillo College, California, 16, *83*, 131–36

California State University(ies), transfer agreements with, 31, 33, 80

California State University at Chico, *31*
CBT (computer-based test), 52
certificate(s), community college, 15–16
Certificate of Eligibility (Form I-20), 50–51, 58–59, 85
choosing a community college, 23–24, 26–44
    academic and career goals, and, 27–28, 121
    accreditation and SEVP certification, and, 28–30, 45
    common mistakes made when, 38–49
    location, cost of living, and, 35–38, 121–22
    transfer partnerships, and, 30–33 (*see also* transfer
partnerships)
    tuition and fees, and, 33–35 (*see also* tuition and fees)
citizenship, American, 110
College Level Examination Program (CLEP) exams, 79–80
Colorado Mountain College, Colorado, 17, 77, 84, 136–40
community college(s), 14–18
    applying to (*see* admission, applying for)
    choosing (*see* choosing a community college)
    enrolling (see enrolling in community college)
    maintaining visa status, 85–86
    reasons for studying at, 18–22
    researching, 22–23, 54–55
    steps toward studying at, 22–24
conditional admission, 54
continuing education units (CEU), 17
Cornell University, 40, 41
cost of living, 19, 35–37, 121–22
courses, 81–83
credit cards, 91–92
credit unions, 90
culture shock, 117–19
currency, 89
Curricular Practical Training (CPT), 103
Customs Declaration (form CF-6059), 68

De Anza College, California, 33, 46–47
debit cards, 91
Designated School Official (DSO), 45, 58, 77
Direct Transfer Agreement (DTA), Washington, 31
disabled students, 21
dormitories, 35, 76
driver's license, 59, 98–99

early action, 47–48
early decision, 47
Edmonds Community College, Washington, 74
EIKEN Test in Practical English Proficiency, 52
Electronic System for Travel Authorization (ESTA), 71
emergencies, 102
employment, 21, 103–5
    Optional Practical Training, 8, 21, 103
employment authorization (form I-765), 104
engineering studies, 40
English-language proficiency, proving, 52–54, 78, 79
English-language skills, improving, 8, 20, 39
enrolling in community college, 76–85
    academic advising and, 81–84
    housing upon arrival, 76–77
    orientation and registration, 84–85
    providing immunization documents, 77
    summary of, 76
    taking assessment tests, 77–79
    taking optional CLEP and AP exams, 79–81
environmental science studies, 40
ESL (English as a Second Language) class, 53
ESTA (Electronic System for Travel Authorization), 71

finances. See funding
financial aid, 35, 49–50
flights, domestic U.S., 72

form(s), 50–52
    CF-6059, 68
    DS-160, 60–61, 62
    I-20, 50–51, 58–59, 85
    I-94, 69–70
    I-134, 49, 76
    I-515A, 70
    I-765, 104
    I-901, 58–59
four-year college and university rankings, 27
funding, 35
    financial aid as 35, 49–50
    providing proof of sufficient, 48–50
    scholarships as, 50

General Education Diploma (GED), 14, 17
goals, academic and career, 27–28
grade point average (GPA), 85
Greyhound bus, travel by, 72–73

Harper College, Illinois, 40, 84
health care and health insurance, 101–2
Highline Community College, Washington, 31, 53
holidays, 112–13
homestays, 35–36, 95
Hopper, David, 64
housing, 35–36, 76–77, 95–96

iBT (internet-based test), 52
IELTS (International English Language Testing System), 52
Illinois Articulation Initiative, 32, 40
immunization, providing proof of, 52, 77
insurance, 99, 101–2
international students
    commentary by, 155–75

common mistakes made by, 38–39
culture shock affecting, 117–19
funding of, 35 (*see also* funding)
most popular fields of study for, 7
national origins of, 7
internet access, 96–97
internships, 104
iTEP (International Test of English Proficiency), 52

Kaskaskia College, Illinois, 40
Kingsborough Community College, New York, 35, 41, 52, 82

letters of recommendation, 51
life in the United States, 89–107
    employment, 103–5
    health care and emergencies, 101–2
    housing, 35–36, 76–77, 95–96
    money matters, 89–92
    shopping, 99–101
    telephone, television, internet, 96–97
    time and dates, 93–95
    transportation, 97–99
loans for tuition, 35

Ma, Yo-Yo, 109
Mass Transfer program, Massachusetts, 32
Mesa Community College, Arizona, 53
money, currency, and banking, 89–92

Normandale Community College, Minnesota, 78
Northern Virginia Community College, Virginia, 31–32, 34, 84
Numbeo.com, 121–22

Obama, Barack, 109
on-campus and off-campus jobs, 103–4

Optional Practical Training (OPT), 8, 21, 103
orientation, 84–85

passport, 24, 51–52
PayPal, 92
PBT (paper-based test), 52
Pima Community College, Arizona, 21, 32, 35, 41, 78, 84, 140–46
placement tests, 53, 77–79
plagiarism, 117
PTE Academic test, 52

registration, 84–85
rolling admissions, 46

San Francisco, California, travel from, to Wyoming, 71–72
Santa Barbara City College, California, 35, 47, 52, 53, 78
Santa Monica College, California, 47, 82–83
scholarships, 50
Secondary Inspection Form I-515A, 70
SEVIS. *See* Student and Exchange Visitor Information System
SEVP. *See* Student and Exchange Visitor Program
shopping, 99–101
Shoreline Community College, Washington, 53
shuttles, transport by, 73–74
Social Security number, 59, 105
space science/astronomy studies, 41
STEM fields, 7
Student and Exchange Visitor Information System (SEVIS), 30, 59
Student and Exchange Visitor Program (SEVP), 23
    certification by, 28, 29–30, 45
    visa application and I-20 form, 58–59
student housing, 35–36, 76–77, 95–96
student life, 76–88

technical colleges, 14–18

telephone service, 96–97

television, 97

time and date conventions, 93–95

TOEFL (Test of English as a Foreign Language), 52–53, 54, 78

tourism and hospitality industry studies, 41

train, travel within U.S. on, 73

transcripts, 51

Transfer Admission Guarantee (TAG), California, 31, 40

transfer partnerships, 21, 30–33, 40, 121

transportation, 37, 38, 71–74, 97–99

travel within the United States, 71–74

tuition and fees, 19, 33–35, 85, 85

2 + 2 degree program, 9–10

United States

    arrival procedures, 68–70

    educational system, 12–18

    holidays, 112–13

    living in (see life in the United States)

    people and culture of, 108–17

    time zones, 93

    travel within, 71–74

U.S. Citizenship and Immigration Services, 49, 104

U.S. Customs and Border Protection, 63, 65

    arrival in U.S. and role of, 68, 69, 70, 71

U.S. Department of Homeland Security, 50, 58, 69, 85

U.S. Department of State, 58, 60, 64

U.S. Immigration and Customs Enforcement (ICE), 58, 59

University of Arizona, Tucson, 32, 41

University(ies) of California, transfer partnerships with, 31, 33, 40

University of California, Berkeley, 33

University of California, Davis, 40

University of California, Santa Cruz, 41

University of Illinois, Urbana-Champaign, 32, 40

University of Michigan, Ann Arbor, 40

University of Texas, Austin, 19, 40, 127
University Transfer program, Florida, 32
utilities and utility bills, 90, 96

vaccinations, 52, 77
Valencia College, Florida, 28, 32, 46, 52, 80, 146–50
Virginia Community College System, 32
visa(s), 24, 58–67
    applying for, 59–63
    denial of, 64
    forms I-20 and I-901, 58–59
    maintaining status, 64–65, 85–86
    sample, *63*
    types of, 59–60
visa interview, 61, 62–63
visa photo, 60–61, 62
Visa Waiver Program, 65, 71
vocational training, 15

Washtenaw Community College, Michigan, 78, 150–54
weather, 38
Western Wyoming Community College, Wyoming, 52, 71–72
working. *See* employment

PHOTO CREDITS

ACKNOWLEDGEMENTS

My sincerest thanks go to everyone who helped me on this project. I especially want to thank those students who took time to answer my questions about their experiences at an American community college. Thanks also go to staff and faculty members who provided photos and information about their respective community colleges. A special thanks goes to Yan Xu at Pima Community College, Tucson, for freely sharing her comprehensive knowledge and experience, and for her photos. Many thanks go to Lynne East-Itkin (lmeastdesign.com) for cover graphic design, and Diane C. Taylor for excellent proofreading.

My hope is that more international students will come to America to study, and more Americans will go abroad to study. I'm convinced that this exchange will lead to greater international understanding and cooperation.

ABOUT THE AUTHOR

C.J. Shane is a journalist, artist, teacher, and traveler. She is a former news reporter, freelance writer, academic reference librarian, professor of library and information science, and an award-winning artist and art critic. She is the author of several books, among them *Voices of New China* (2013). Learn more at cjshane.com

Made in the USA
San Bernardino, CA
20 April 2017